THE POWER OF THOUGHT

THE
POWER
OF THOUGHT

Ageless Secrets of Great Achievement

GLENN BLAND

PRIMA PUBLISHING

PRIMA PUBLISHING and colophon are trademarks of Prima Communications, Inc.

Library of Congress Cataloging-in-Publication Data

Bland, Glenn.
   The power of thought : ageless secrets of great achievement / by Glenn Bland.
      p.   cm.
   Includes index.
   ISBN 0-7615-0341-2
   1. Success.   I. Title.
BJ1611.2.B555 1995
158'.1—dc20   95-36034
                                                                     CIP

96 97 98 99 00 DD 10 9 8 7 6 5 4 3 2 1
Printed in the United States of America

How to Order:

Single copies may be ordered from Prima Publishing, P.O. Box 1260BK, Rocklin, CA 95677; telephone (916) 632-4400. Quantity discounts are also available. On your letterhead, include information concerning the intended use of the books and the number of books you wish to purchase.

To my beloved grandchildren:
Leesa Grace Jensen
Lawrence Keith "Luke" Jensen, Jr.
Mary Bland Jensen
Joseph Vernon Bland, Jr.
Glenn David Bland

And to:
Richard Glenn Chandler
Gary Glenn Wells

Other Books by Glenn Bland

Legend of the Golden Scrolls: Ageless Secrets for Building Wealth, Prima Publishing, P.O. Box 1260BK, Rocklin, CA 95677, (916) 632-4400

Success: The Glenn Bland Method, Tyndale House Publishers, P.O. Box 80, Wheaton, IL 60189-0080, (708) 668-8300

Contents

Acknowledgments   ix
Preface   xi

I: The Power of Thought

Dreams   3
Purpose   19
Effort   31
Responsibility   41
Circumstances   51
Character   67
Faith   77
Balance   97

II: Classic Quotations

The Power of Words   113

Index   155

Acknowledgments

In sincere appreciation to Verna Beth Bland and Deborah Huff for their invaluable assistance. To Ebbie, Lanny, Ronny, Ross and Royce for their priceless gift.

Preface

Each chapter of this work reveals a secret regarding a specific vital element of great achievement. Without mastering these, no person can attain true success or the happiness, meaning, fulfillment, serenity and prosperity that go along with it.

Throughout the last three decades, I have had the privilege of tutoring hundreds of salespeople during the initial years in which they developed their careers. Many of them became my close friends. I knew their spouses and children. On special occasions, we socialized and enjoyed various kinds of recreation. We were like one big family. Some placed me in the position of patriarch and shared their innermost feelings with me.

Most of those in the family circle became very successful, but some failed. I can honestly say that not one of those who failed did so out of lack of intelligence or ability. To the contrary, I found them to be most capable. The reason they failed was that they would not subscribe to the discipline of the way that successful people think. They were stiff-necked and chose to do things their own way, even though it meant certain failure.

During the same period, I took it upon myself to study the careers of some of the great achievers of history. I searched for common attributes and philosophies to find the secrets of their extraordinary success. My research proved most enlightening.

Among those whose careers I analyzed were Andrew Carnegie, W. Edwards Deming, Richard De Vos, Thomas

A. Edison, Ben Feldman, Henry Ford, Lou Gehrig, J. Paul Getty, Billy Graham, Lee Iacocca, Michael Jordan, Mary Kay, Helen Keller, Martin Luther King, Jr., Tom Landry, Abraham Lincoln, Norman Vincent Peale, John D. Rockefeller, Theodore Roosevelt, Norman Schwartzkoff, Albert Schweitzer, W. Clement Stone, Margaret Thatcher, and Jay Van Andel.

I discovered that these notable people all shared certain characteristics and opinions, even though their backgrounds were vastly different. These special threads of similarity elevated them to greatness.

During the same three decades, I explored the Sacred Scriptures in search of wisdom which would shed more light on the essential traits of great achievers. In-depth studies of the lives of Moses, David, Solomon, Jesus and Paul revealed the same essential traits of greatness that I discovered in the other people whose careers I had analyzed.

In time, my investigative inquiry into the lives of great achievers led me to the conclusion that special human qualities exist that when developed and employed ensure extraordinary accomplishment. These special qualities may be learned and utilized by any individual who possesses a genuine desire to become highly successful.

Few people have had a more difficult upbringing than me. Scarcity, fear and abuse were common. A bitter divorce ravaged my boyhood. The streets became my sanctuary. I lived alone throughout my teens. Daily troubles consumed me. Negativism permeated my life. Vivid memories of these vexing years are indelibly written in my heart.

Out of those abhorrent circumstances, my desire for a better life grew. That desire compelled me to discover the personal qualities that ensure success. I developed and employed these special qualities myself and built one of the largest marketing companies of its kind in America. I simply applied what I learned, and the positive results took care of themselves. If I can do it, believe me, you can do it!

All of the secrets of great achievement that eminent people have known about for millenniums are disclosed throughout the following pages. You will discover a new way to think and act that literally guarantees success. You will discern how I, as well as the many people I have tutored, have achieved my dreams. You will perceive just what it takes to reach your full potential. You will conceive a way to shape and mold your life, making it all that you want it to be. You will gain the wisdom to grasp the true significance of Solomon's aphorism, "As a man thinks in his heart, so is he."

Throughout the text, I chose to use the masculine gender to best facilitate the writing of this work. The context in which it is used is completely applicable to the feminine gender as well. Fortunately, the vital elements of great achievement are gender neutral.

Go forward now and begin the quest that will ensure a permanent place for you among those rare individuals who attain true success. The secrets of great achievement await your discovery.

G.D.B.
Memphis, Tennessee

PART I

THE POWER OF THOUGHT

Chapter 1

DREAMS

He whom a dream hath possessed
knoweth no more of doubting.
　　—Sharmas O'Sheel

The dreamer who takes action and develops unwavering faith becomes the mover of mountains. A dream is like a mustard seed: when it is sown, it is the smallest of all garden seeds, but as it is nurtured and grows to maturity, it becomes the largest of all garden plants. The nurturing process requires care on the part of the gardener, for his garden must be cultivated, weeded, and watered. That nurturing process also requires the gardener to have faith—unwavering faith to persevere until harvest time.

Dreamers achieve all sorts of successful careers. They are clergymen, businessmen, statesmen, salesmen, executives, entrepreneurs, inventors, scientists, physicians, teachers, artists, writers, composers. Their dreams affect the lives of laboring humanity and give everyone the opportunity to rise above a base existence. Their dreams serve as beacons of enlightenment that illuminate the way for others to follow. The man who envisions a captivating dream and embraces it perpetually in his heart will see it come to fruition. A cherished dream gives rise to purpose, and purpose brings goals to bear. The pursuit of definite goals necessitates having a plan of action. The man with well-defined goals and a plan for their accomplishment will see his purpose realized and his dream fulfilled, just as sure as the seasons come and go.

In early 1959, Jay Van Andel and Richard De Vos met in a basement office in Van Andel's home in Ada, Michigan. In that modest place the seeds of the world's greatest private business enterprise were sown. They conceived a dream to build a thriving network marketing company. Their dream crystallized into an all-consuming purpose, which they transformed into definite goals and plans. It was to be a people business that promoted entrepreneurial spirit and free enterprise. It would be founded upon sound principles that, if followed, ensured success. It would be a venture that conducted its affairs in the truest sense of the American Way.

There were endless days and nights of decision making, defining goals, making plans, developing administrative procedures, creating products, conducting meetings, and recruiting, training, and motivating independent distributors. Van Andel and De Vos were enthusiastic. They believed in themselves. They worked as though their very lives depended on it. "I can" was their slogan.

Today, that original dream has grown into the gigantic Amway Corporation. Thousands of independent Amway distributors, located throughout much of the world, have achieved their own success stories. Some have become millionaires. All work for themselves and are building better and more rewarding lives. The Amway story is profound proof that dreams can make the accomplishments of ordinary people extraordinary. It is out of the dreams of men that all accomplishment materializes.

Most great dreamers emerge from humble beginnings. Such was the case with Martin Luther King Jr., a Georgia Baptist minister who passionately dreamed of fulfilling the biblical principle of life, liberty, and the pursuit of happiness for every man, woman, and child living in America. He believed that the forefathers granted these fundamental rights to each citizen in the Declaration of Independence.

Being a wise and prudent man, Martin Luther King understood that Americans are fortunate to be born in this great land. He realized that there is no other nation like it on the face of the earth. Why? Because the framers of the Constitution sagaciously gave the citizenry principal power to govern themselves through duly elected representatives who would serve in a federal capacity. They also ordained that all citizens must be treated alike under the law. They established a free society in which an individual can rise as high and go as far as his legitimate dreams impel him. They provided the framework for genuine democracy and free enterprise through an ingenious document that is so indefectible it is suggestive of divine inspiration.

Martin Luther King Jr. found no fault with the Constitution. Instead, he praised it as a unique instrument of freedom. But he did find fault with a society that did not exercise the comprehensiveness of the Constitution in regard to every race, color, and creed. He condemned society for its double standard, in which some men were more free than others. He said, "Nothing in the world is more dangerous than sincere ignorance and conscientious stupidity." His statement constituted an apt characterization of the American society of his day.

Dr. King was the namesake of Martin Luther, who led the Protestant Reformation of the early 1500s, which changed religion on the Eurasian continent. It was fitting that his namesake should lead what was perhaps the most sweeping social reformation of the North American continent. Destiny called, and he answered.

Martin Luther King Jr. was a dreamer. He said, "I have a dream that my four little children will one day live in a nation where they will not be judged by the color of their skin, but by the content of their character." His dream translated into an all-inclusive purpose, which inspired definite goals and detailed plans and action! His was a total commitment. In this regard, he said, "If a man hasn't discovered something that he will die for, he isn't fit to live." Every man, so dedicated, shall make his dream materialize.

The Baptist minister's dream was intense and vividly clear. It aroused his emotions and titillated his psyche. He fervently declared, "I just want to do God's will. And He's allowed me to go up to the mountain. And I've looked over, and I've seen the Promised Land"—a biblical reference to Moses standing atop Pisgah Peak of Mount Nebo and seeing the land of Canaan. Every dreamer has a mountain to climb before he actually sees the Promised Land.

Dr. King's enthusiasm and conviction grew contagious and infected the minds of others who consciously chose to follow his dream as their own. They too spoke of Constitutional liberty—the kind that treats every individual equally under the laws of the land and provides each citizen with the equal opportunity to succeed or fail and to willingly accept full responsibility for the outcome. Their zealous dream first became a cause, and then it developed into a movement that transcended the lifespan of its founder, as well as many of the early enthusiasts who helped make it a reality.

Today that dream is coming to fruition. Many individuals are building successful lives on the foundation that was laid by Dr. King and his dedicated followers. The fulfillment of this dream is producing new human resources for entrepreneurship, business, labor, politics, government, academe, religion, medicine, science, industry, athletics, entertainment, and art. Many others will rise to high places also, once they too discover how to think as successful people think and apply principles that reward them with dreams fulfilled. To rise to great heights of achievement they must ascend on the magical wings of the power of thought.

Because Martin Luther King was a man of principle, which stemmed from his knowledge of the Sacred Scriptures, his continuing vision would have had no limit. Once the initial phase of his dream was realized—the creation of equal opportunity for every American—he would have then initiated a second phase. He had a masterful understanding of Solomon's aphorism "As a man thinketh in his heart [mind], so is he," a profound precept that comes from the Book of Proverbs in the Old Testament.

Based on this principle, King would have wisely exhorted his followers to nurture their fertile minds and learn how to utilize the power of thought. Properly directed thoughts are the seeds of all personal growth and achievement. The cultivation of the mind is essential to meritorious accomplishment. A literate mind knows only the boundaries that it imposes on itself.

The laws of the land may set men free in the physical sense, but unless individuals take it upon themselves to cultivate their minds, they shall remain in psychic bondage. This groveling mental state is as repressive as physical enslavement, and those who succumb to it can rise no higher than their limitative thoughts will permit them to go.

But those who dream of a better life and consciously choose to cultivate their minds shall find freedom in its truest sense. Unfortunately, principled mental growth is something that individuals must acquire for themselves, something that others cannot acquire for them. Those fortunate individuals who cultivate their minds will elevate their thoughts, and their material environment shall change accordingly.

True success is the handiwork of rightly directed principled thought. Individuals who earnestly desire the best that life has to offer must willingly exchange their old thoughts for different thoughts—thoughts that have withstood the test of time and that have directed others who achieved true success. It is important to learn from the experiences of those who live by principle instead of the dictates of emotion, relativism, and materialism.

Choose those that you emulate carefully, for their destiny shall be yours also. Better yet, study and learn the principles of *true* success on your own, and thus you will become your own person. Principled people are the real successes of this confused age.

Lasting prosperity will not bless individuals who fail to prepare themselves to receive it. Preparation requires learning the laws that govern prosperity —laws that actually attract riches when they are applied to the daily enterprise of life.

A man does not acquire enduring wealth through folly, luck, or chance. Instead, he finds it through the ongoing application of the laws, which verify the value of specialized knowledge, dreams, purpose, goals, plans, effort, thrift, and patience. The way to prosperity is no longer mysterious to those who find it, but it remains an enigma to those who are ignorant of the laws.

Being a learned man who recognized infinite truth, Dr. King understood that although each citizen has certain inalienable rights, every mortal is an innately unique creation. Each is endowed with distinct intelligence and ability unlike any other individual. Each possesses unique degrees of potential and limitation. Each has specific likes and dislikes. No person is the exact duplicate of another, even though individuals may share common interests. This is the miracle of divine creation.

Common logic dictates that individuals must seek their own niches within the strata of society, for finding their rightful places is essential to their happiness and fulfillment. A healthy, thriving nation must have citizens involved within the numerous levels of society that contribute to the whole. The uniqueness of individuals who have varying abilities and interests accommodates the needs of the whole.

In America, individuals are free to choose how and where they can serve society best within the homogeneity of their own dreams. This is why the American society produces such abundant opportunities for individual citizens as laborers, managers, owners, professionals, and capitalists alike. All are needed, all are vital to the success of the whole.

The vision of Martin Luther King Jr. was far-reaching. It projected a future in which equal opportunity was available to every individual regardless of his race, color, or creed, to a time when every individual would come to know the greatness of the American Dream and willingly participate in it, when all able-bodied Americans would forego being on the perpetual government or private-charity dole, in favor of the challenge of personal accomplishment and healthy self-esteem.

Today, opportunity abounds for any dreamer who is willing to pay the price of success. Other phases of Dr. King's dream are still in the making. They will come to fruition once those individuals who are plagued by misguided agendas and skepticism discover that every person is an independent creative force who is capable of making his own dreams come true. For bringing equal opportunity to bear, this remarkable man must be awarded the irrefutable credit for a truly worthy dream realized.

Some individuals envision dreams that are seemingly impossible to realize. Such is the inspiring story of the meteoric rise of Margaret Thatcher to official prominence in Great Britain. Her dream was seemingly impossible because she chose to hitch her wagon to what was predominantly a gentlemen's world: politics. Only a highly motivated visionary with limitless intestinal fortitude would have undertaken such a difficult challenge. Only a person driven by passion and principle would have believed that the improbable quest could have ended successfully. Only a courageous woman would have looked the devil straight in the eye and then defeated him on his own battlefield.

The underlying motive for Margaret Thatcher's decision to enter the political arena was her fervent love for her country. She feared that big government and creeping socialism would eventually destroy the fiber of the nation if measures were not taken to curtail their growth. She, like Sir Winston Churchill before her, believed socialism to be no more than the equal sharing of misery. She was an aggressive defender of capitalism and a staunch advocate of the free market. Being intensely independent herself, she fiercely supported the right of individual freedom. These were the issues that she enthusiastically fought for during her ascent up the political ladder.

Mrs. Thatcher was elected to Parliament in 1959. She immediately gained the respect of the opposition, as well as her peers, because of her intelligence, political savvy, and dynamic leadership qualities. She spoke her convictions and was genuinely respected for it. In 1975, she replaced Edward Heath as the Conservative party leader, which was her springboard to becoming England's first female prime minister in 1979. And a great prime minister she was.

Margaret Thatcher initiated a new monetary policy that curtailed rampant inflation by reducing the money supply and eliminating gratuitous social programs. In 1982, her good judgment and decisiveness repelled Argentina's attempt to seize the Falkland Islands through armed conflict. The British military lion roared and responded immediately, halting the Argentinean invasion and bringing the war to a quick conclusion. Her belief in a free market prompted her to sell many state-owned enterprises; that action had a very positive impact on the economy during the mid and late 1980s. In foreign policy, she was a strong ally of the United States.

Mrs. Thatcher was affectionately called the Iron Lady because of her dauntless leadership and unquestionable character. She capably served as the prime minister of the British Empire for a longer time than anyone else in the twentieth century. Following her retirement from the House of Commons in 1992, she was royally appointed Baroness Thatcher of Kesteven.

Margaret Thatcher achieved her seemingly impossible dream. What appeared to be impossible to others appeared vividly possible to her. She patiently nurtured her dream in her heart, all the while believing that, at the proper moment in the great universal scheme of things, it would come to fruition. It did, and she became prime minister. Dreams come true for individuals who possess childlike faith —the kind that Jesus spoke of that is so powerful it can move mountains.

To dream is to envision. To envision is to act. To act is to achieve. Can a low-minded, vile man ever find complete fulfillment while forsaking worthy aspirations and purity of heart? Never, for he defies Higher Law. He forfeits the blessing of "Ask and you will be given what you ask for." He relinquishes the "peace, which is far more wonderful than the human mind can understand."

The great challenge of life is to dream grand dreams of noble substance and to hold those dreams dear, for they are the fabric from which the future will be woven —an exciting future, teeming with golden possibilities.

The highest achievements of men started as the seed of their dreams. A single acorn grows into a thousand forests. A grain of corn multiplies and plants many fields. One grapevine produces thousands of grapes. Dreams are the seeds of all future realities.

A son was born to the wife of a carpenter whose living conditions were scant and wanting. His boyhood was occupied by long hours, day after day, assisting his earthly father in the family business. He received no formal education. He was not schooled in the arts. He was never taught the skills of social refinement. Not once did he ever sit at the feet of the master teachers of distinction.

In his limited circumstances, he dreamed of a higher calling, one that required him to think, to study, and to develop refinement and grace. He grew to maturity, replete with love and beauty within.

His dream evolved into a purpose, and his purpose grew into a mission, a mission that consumed him, creating restlessness and impelling him to act. So strong was the burning desire within that the carpenter shop was no longer of interest to him. Therefore, he laid his tools aside and followed the conviction of his heart.

He set out to make the world a better place. He spoke of God, love, and the brotherhood of man. His intellect astounded even his critics. No one had ever taught as he taught. Multitudes listened and pondered his words, which were uniquely simple and yet much deeper than any man had ever spoken. Lives were changed. Kings took notice. His popularity and influence increased prodigiously. His fame, heightened by his supernatural exploits, knew no boundaries.

The responsibility that he held was of awesome proportions. The power that he assumed was unparalleled in

history. Yet, he never once misused his position, nor took
advantage of a single person. He left mankind a valuable
legacy for both time and eternity. His contributions to the
human race have no equal.

The youth of meager circumstances became the quin-
tessential figure of history. It is unlikely that any library in
the world would hold all of the many volumes that have
been written about him. He fulfilled his dream. He
achieved his purpose.

These profound words of Richard De Vos reveal in
beautifully simple terms the sum and substance of the
mystery of success and failure: "Those people whose aim
is always low generally hit what they shoot at: they aim
for nothing and hit it. Life need not be lived that way. I
believe that one of the most powerful forces in the world
is the will of the man who believes in himself, who dares
to aim high, to go confidently after the things that he
wants from life."

Unknowing people, envious bystanders, and jealous
onlookers who do not fathom the power of dreams attribute the success of others to special fortune or unscrupulous practices. Such critics judge dreamers who
grow rich according to their own limited perspectives,
ethical persuasions, and moral orientations. They are
blind to the truth because of their failure to learn of it.
They are bound to their unprincipled circumstances by
their own thoughts. In ignorance, they cast stones at
those who achieve greatly.

Such critics cannot comprehend the vision, commitment, planning, effort, challenge, and persistence necessary to the success of a worthy enterprise. They are void
of understanding the many sacrifices that were made.

They are unaware of the numerous obstacles that were overcome. They are oblivious to the risk, concern, disappointment, and heartache encountered. They know nothing of the lengthy journey and the patience to endure. They see only the ultimate reward and judge it to be achieved by special favor, chance, or luck.

Theodore Roosevelt, a visionary who well understood the frequent judgments that dreamers become subjected to, said this: "It is not the critic who counts, not the man who points out how the strong man stumbles, or where the doer of deeds could have done them better. The credit belongs to the man who is actually in the arena, whose face is marred by dust and sweat and blood, who strives valiantly, who errs and comes short again and again because there is no effort without error and shortcoming, but who does actually strive to do the deeds, who knows the great enthusiasms, the great devotions, who spends himself in a worthy cause, who at the best knows in the end the triumph of high achievement and who at the worst, if he fails, at least fails while daring greatly, so that his place shall never be with those cold and timid souls who know neither victory or defeat."

Truth decrees that human beings cannot escape the omnipotence of the Law of Cause and Effect, for it is omnipresent and immutable. The millionaire, the worker, the beggar are equally subject to its rule. Each has reached his particular station in life because of this law, which ensures that each man receives that which he has justly earned.

Effort, or cause, produces reward, or effect. The greater the effort expended, the greater the reward gained. Special favor, chance, and luck are null in the

universal scheme of things. All achievement, or the lack
thereof, is the reward of effort, or the need of it. In
essence, success or failure are thoughts manifested,
dreams attained, purpose actualized.

Get yourself a dream. Hold fast to it. Cherish it as
though it is pure gold. Let it stir your heart and stimulate
your mind, for out of your dream will grow the future
conditions of your life. Follow your dream faithfully, and
it will one day be realized.

Today your circumstances may be burdensome and
difficult, but such conditions will be short-lived if you just
conceive a challenging dream and pursue it with all your
heart. As your dream changes your inner world of
thought, your outer world of circumstance will respond
and change also. A soul-stirring dream is an agent of
change.

Be prudent regarding what you consciously dream
about, for it will come to pass. The dream that you exalt
in your thoughts and cherish in your heart is the foun-
tainhead for a lifetime of successful achievement.

You will one day fulfill the dream that you harbor in
your heart. It will come to fruition regardless of its nature : evil or good or a combination of both, it makes no
difference. Your life will eventually manifest what you in-
timately desire the most. You will receive the true rewards
for your effort, in exact kind and measure as the characteristics of your own thoughts.

Regardless of your present station in life, you will accept the status quo, succeed, or fail in direct relation to
the essence of your thoughts. You will rise as high as your
preeminent dream or descend as low as your most base

imagination. Because of your freedom to think as you choose, the future direction of your life is therefore in your hands. You alone are responsible.

❖ POWER THOUGHT ❖

Your vision is the signet of your destiny.

Chapter 2

Purpose

Great minds have purposes, others have wishes.
　—Washington Irving

When Albert Schweitzer was asked, "What is wrong with men today?" the great doctor replied, "They simply do not think." His profound answer reveals the root of the mediocrity that afflicts the masses. People who fail to devote adequate time to the business of thinking fall woefully short of reaching their potential. Many dream of crystal palaces and streets of gold, but few ever translate their dreams into purpose because purpose requires painstaking thought. Purpose is the moving force behind all achievement. A definite purpose, conceived through productive thought, creates energy capable of uncommon accomplishment.

The legendary J. Paul Getty thought of riches and purposed to find his fortune in black gold under the red clay of eastern Oklahoma. "I served a tough and valuable apprenticeship working as a roustabout and tool dresser in the oil fields," he said, confirming that he gave himself adequate time to learn the oil business from the bottom up. In 1914, he decided to forgo his regular paycheck and try his luck at discovering black gold as an independent operator—a wildcatter. The risks were astronomical, but the potential rewards were staggering.

Getty's first year on his own was anything but profitable. New gushers came in regularly for others, but costly dry holes troubled him. This was indeed a discouraging predicament since his operating capital was almost depleted. In the late fall of 1915, he bought half the interest in a Muskogee County oil lease for the bargain price of five hundred dollars. Having no money to invest in the venture, he formed a corporation of investors in which he retained only fifteen percent interest. The drilling began, and the acute stress he encountered day after day was almost impossible to bear. He literally sweated out every foot of hole that the drilling bit dug deep into the earth.

As the late afternoon shadows lengthened across the prairie and the chilling wintry wind bent the brown tall grass southward, a deep rumbling sound emitted from the mouth of the well's casing. Only seconds later black gold blew the drilling bit through the crown of the wooden derrick with such force that the thick beams snapped like penny matchsticks. Rich, inky oil shot up more than a hundred feet into the air, spraying everything in the area with a slick film of liquid treasure. The gusher produced thirty barrels an hour.

Getty sold his fifteen percent interest in the oil well for $12,000, which represented enough working capital for him to continue as a wildcatter, pursuing his purpose of acquiring wealth. From that point on, he struck oil more often than not. Success blessed him abundantly. His purpose compelled him to become the world's first billionaire and a legend during his lifetime.

People whose thoughts are aimless and whose lives lack purpose are subject to folly, uncertainty, cynicism, hardship, subjugation, and self-pity. Consequently, their rewards are shallowness, fear, dissatisfaction, misfortune, bondage, and delusion. It is indeed perilous to wander through life without the benefit of substantive thought linked with legitimate purpose.

Scott Applewhite demonstrated extraordinary potential for future success in his youth. He was intelligent enough, but his best assets were his athletic prowess and social skills, which he learned to exploit to his advantage. Honors and popularity came easily. He manipulated both people and conditions and always got what he wanted. He coasted through college, putting forth minimal effort to earn his diploma.

If Applewhite had a fundamental weakness, it was that his interests were extremely diverse. He never remained focused on anything very long. His opinions vacillated. He continuously switched from one college major to another. He hippety-hopped between friends constantly. Every serious relationship was short-lived. Even his recreational activities changed frequently. The blessing of versatility was also his nemesis.

After college, Applewhite quickly became dissatisfied with working for an international banking conglomerate. He moved to the West Coast in search of a job more to his liking. As the years slipped by, he tried numerous things— coaching, acting, real estate sales, hotel management, commercial fishing, foreign importing—but he quit each undertaking. His venture into foreign importing brought him into direct contact with underworld characters who made millions smuggling illegal drugs from Columbia to the United States. They used the legitimate export business as a front to cover up their criminal activities. They coaxed Applewhite to join them with the devilish promise of instant riches. He liked the idea.

The first shipment of cocaine that Applewhite received was hidden in the false ends of three wooden crates filled with leather goods. The small shipment made him $21,000 selling the drugs on the street. It was just enough money to increase his enthusiasm for drug dealing. The next shipment was larger—$1 million street value. This would be his first really big score.

Applewhite had already uncrated the plastic bags of cocaine and stacked them high on a freight dolly when FDA agents suddenly broke in and arrested him, confiscating the evidence that would be instrumental in putting him away in a federal prison for most of his remaining life. Eight days following his fifty-sixth birthday, he was released from custody to return to society a sick and broken man. He died just a few months later.

This is an example of a life void of constructive thought and definite purpose. Scott Applewhite possessed intelligence and ability, but he failed to utilize his gifts in a concentrated, worthwhile way. He had no well-thought-out purpose and therefore became vulnerable to joining in the purposes of others. He survived as long as the purposes of others were honorable, but when he joined a mob having criminal purposes, the relationship destroyed his life. By drifting through life without a definite, worthwhile purpose, he left himself open to unprincipled ideas that tempted him so intensely he eventually acquiesced.

The carpenter from Nazareth achieved numerous goals and fulfilled numerous plans, but behind all of his success was the power of a great dream, which he transformed into a single compelling purpose: to redeem mankind. His compulsion was so strong that at age thirty he put aside his hammer, saw, square, and plane and left his family to undertake the challenge of revealing his Heavenly Father to his fellow man. His message was soul-stirring and dynamic. His life was a perfect example of godliness. He made the world a better place by changing the hearts of sinful men. He gave people hope and enthusiasm for living. He treated all men with equal respect and love.

Yet he suffered ridicule, disloyalty, prejudice, deceit, malice, and mental and physical abuse from friends, religious leaders, and government officials. At age thirty-three, in exemplary innocence, he was nailed to a Roman cross to bear the most agonizing death known to man. As he hung there in excruciating pain and unmitigated humiliation, he prayed for the forgiveness of all those responsible for his tragic circumstances.

Although he did no wrong, he was wronged, but out of his adversity emerged the redemption of men for both time and eternity. His purpose required that he pay the ultimate price, an act of love for mankind having no equivalent.

A true sense of purpose creates an energy that manifests itself in the form of motivation from within—motivation so forceful that it drives you to action. All forms of external motivation, although sometimes helpful, are short-lived because their essence prevents them from being internalized. Their effects may be beneficial for the moment, but they soon dissipate into nothingness and leave you none for the better. Conversely, motivation from within flows from a deep inner fountain, which is perennial.

If you earnestly desire to achieve greatness, conceive a dream, turn it into a compelling purpose, and then pursue it vigorously. Focus on it each day. Make it your passion. Let it live in your heart, and in the proper season it shall come to pass.

Purpose is that silent, tugging force within that pulls you out, freeing you from your negative self, giving you the undying will to succeed. It is that all-consuming something that preoccupies your mind. It is the reason that you define specific goals and plans. It is your motive for total commitment, hard work, and perseverance.

Purpose is the abiding creed that arises from the distillation of your dream. It is the all-inclusive statement of your calling. It is that special thought that makes your adrenaline surge, breath quicken, heart pound, and reserve energy enliven your being. It is the primary reason you get out of bed each morning to greet the new day with enthusiasm.

You must make your purpose a major priority in your life. Cultivate it. Cherish it. Embrace it. Focus your attention on its fulfillment. Refrain from distracting and unimportant imaginings. Be true to your purpose, and your purpose will prove true to you.

When obstacles and difficulties obstruct your pathway, demonstrate the tenacity to prevail and trample them in the dust. Staying the course and overcoming such adversities builds character and deepens experience. The challenge of conquering adversities eliminates all those who are not truly committed from the race. The weak-hearted quit and fall by the wayside while the stout-hearted persevere and cross the finish line victorious.

The act of overcoming adversity enhances personal growth. As you creatively conquer each challenge, you will improve your focus, self-control, wisdom, patience, ingenuity, persistence, and faith. In the final analysis, your character maturation constitutes the true measure of your success.

The race begins right where you are today and ends when your purpose is fulfilled. This marathon requires continuous learning, practice, courage, discipline, and in-dustry. Staying the course is grueling and uncompromis-ing, but once you triumphantly cross the finish line amidst thunderous applause, to receive your prize atop the victor's stand, your heart will confirm that the accom-plishment of your purpose was indeed worth the great price that you paid.

The race that the carpenter of Nazareth ran, from his humble beginning to the inauguration of his spiritual kingdom, was exceedingly difficult, but the ultimate result of his commitment greatly overshadows his sacrifice. His accomplishment was so far reaching that it defies both time and eternity. He, standing alone against powerful opposition, achieved his purpose.

The luminaries of religion, scholarship, statesman-ship, business, invention, sports, and the arts are simply common people who achieved an uncommon purpose. The secret of their success lies in the fact that they allowed their purpose to draw them out of the habitual mediocrity of commonness through the application of extraordinary effort and practice. They concentrated on developing their natural abilities.

These luminaries can be found among every race and creed. Many of them emerged from disadvantaged beginnings. Although these people are inherently different, there are some common threads of greatness that link them together:

1. They each have a definite purpose.
2. They perceive obstacles as stepping stones to success.
3. They utilize their circumstances to their best advantage.
4. They are avid practitioners of possibility thinking.

Once you envision your own definite purpose, create detailed goals and plans that will take you the most direct route to its accomplishment. Focus on your agenda every day. Put all of your mental and physical energy into your tasks. Be enthusiastic and believe that you will succeed even when others say you cannot.

During the early development of manned flights, it was considered impossible to fly faster than the speed of sound. The sound barrier was conceived as an obstacle much like a brick wall, thus being impenetrable. However, man did the seemingly impossible and advanced beyond that point to which he thought he could not go.

In the same sense, the masses imagine the existence of a *pain barrier* that stands between them and the fulfillment of their dreams. They think that this barrier is impossible to break and, therefore, most refuse to even try. Consequently, theirs is a lifestyle of limitation and want.

Granted, there is a pain barrier that confronts every achiever, just as the sound barrier once confronted man in flight. The pain barrier is that point on the road to accomplishing your purpose beyond which the way becomes smoother. It is that welcome rung up the ladder of success where tight-fisted struggle ends and good fortune begins. At that special point in the process of personal growth rudimentary suffering ceases, and the benefits of learning and experience start paying rewards. This turning point initiates the transition from scarcity to abundance.

Regardless of your present circumstances, you must persevere long enough to break the pain barrier or you will never accomplish your purpose. When you feel that you have gone your last mile, resolve to go just one more. When you think you have reached the end of that extra mile, muster the courage to go just one more, and when you find that you are nearing its end, go just one more. Keep on going the extra mile even when your enthusiasm wanes, discouragement renders you near helpless, adversity envelops you, and fatigue holds you firmly in its clutches. Never, never, never give up! Stay in the race until you break the pain barrier, and then you will suddenly receive a second wind sufficient enough to triumph and accomplish your purpose.

Fear, doubt, and indecisiveness are disabling conditions that you must overcome, or they will neutralize your commitment and dilute your effort. These psyche-numbing conditions can thwart your success, so you must stand ready to confront and overcome them each time you are challenged. Fear, doubt, and indecisiveness are insidious arch enemies that must be driven from your thoughts again and again until they vacate your mind. As long as you permit them to take residence there, you carry with you seeds of failure that usurp your energy, power, and resolve.

The decision to take action originates from the belief that you will succeed. Confidence and doubt, courage and fear, decisiveness and indecisiveness, cannot coexist in your thoughts. Once you permanently resolve to conquer doubt, fear, and indecisiveness with the belief that you will succeed, you have then conquered failure. Consequently, your belief will beget the power needed to follow the narrow pathway to the fulfillment of your purpose, overcoming every obstacle that you encounter with confidence, courage, and decisiveness.

If you find yourself apprehensive concerning whether you are aptly prepared for the challenges that undertaking a definite purpose brings, have courage and exercise just enough faith to begin. Focus your thoughts on learning and doing the fundamentals well, regardless of how menial your efforts appear. In time, your self-confidence will grow as you gain useful experience. Then be courageous and exercise just enough faith to undertake the next level of achievement. When you reach proficiency at the new level, take courage and exercise just enough faith to progress to the next level. Thus, you will systematically grow in thought, effort, and practice to the level of skill necessary for you to accomplish your purpose.

Even the weakest of men can find the wherewithal necessary to achieve their purpose if they will only concentrate their thoughts, employ consistent effort, and learn through practice. Thought stimulates effort, effort augments practice, and practice bears perfection.

Do you truly desire to be the best you can be at your craft? Then you must consistently do three things: Practice, practice, practice. Greatness is the recompense for practice.

When a soul-stirring dream empowers a definite purpose, a wondrous new energy is created, that prevails over every detail of your quest. This energy transforms its characteristics into power, the unrelenting power to succeed. If you can comprehend and believe in this precept, you are destined to join the distinctive ranks of achievers who determine the outcome of their own lives. You will possess wisdom to discern how dreams and purpose unite to form and shape your environment.

❖ POWER THOUGHT ❖

A definite purpose is a compass for the journey of life.

Chapter 3

EFFORT

Lazy people want much but get little,
while the diligent are prospering.
　—Solomon

Every material reward is the product of effort. The magnitude of a reward is determined by the amount of effort expended. There can be no material reward without sustained, concentrated effort.

Aesop told a thought-provoking fable about a farmer and his sons that is a masterly illustration of how there can be no treasure without toil:

> A farmer, being at death's door and desiring to impart to his sons a secret of much moment, called them around him and said, "My sons, I am shortly about to die. I would have you know, therefore, that in my vineyard there lies a hidden treasure. Dig, and you will find it." As soon as their father was dead, the sons took spade

and fork and turned up the soil of the vineyard over and over again, in their search for the treasure which was supposed to lie buried there. They found none, however; but the vines, after so thorough a digging, produced a crop such as had never before been seen.

Effort is the conscious exertion of energy sufficient to achieve a particular end. Once a man firmly resolves to seek fortune or knowledge or religion or artistic mastery or public service, he then must apply himself wholeheartedly toward the realization of his purpose. In the material world, the greater effort earns the greater reward.

The masses perceive the essence of effort strictly in the physical sense. This is why the consequences of their lives are fraught with limitations. They fail to realize that the true essence of effort is both physical and mental, with greater emphasis on the latter.

Although constructive thinking is difficult, it is the real business of life. In every successful endeavor, a dream crystallized into purpose always precedes effort. Dreams—purpose—effort—reward. That constitutes the established order for all accomplishment.

Imaginative thought is indeed laborious and, thus, fatiguing. This is the reason why so few people do it of their own volition. However, those who do become the leaders, architects, and servants of the entire human experience.

A man never feels more happy and fulfilled than when he has spent himself for the achievement of a noble purpose. He never experiences more satisfaction and serenity than when he sits alone at the evening hour and reflects on each challenging accomplishment that comprised an engaging day of productive effort. Broadway

Joe Namath, the daring New York Jets quarterback, described the extraordinary reward that all-out effort brings in a simple, yet profound way. He said, "When you win, nothing hurts." A brilliant maxim from one who knows both the ecstasy of victory and the misery of hard-fought defeat.

Conversely, a man is never more sad and unfulfilled than when he has spent himself in the pursuit of a worthy purpose and failed. Feeling tired and dejected, he sits alone in the quiet of the evening searching for answers to why he gave his all and lost. The answers elude him. He momentarily thinks of quitting. He wonders if the potential reward is worth the extraordinary price that he must pay. He says to himself, "When you lose, everything hurts." Self-pity and discouragement consume him. He then plunges into the depths of emotional agony and despair.

Every successful man experiences such moments. They temper an iron heart into a heart of steel, leaving it stronger, more enduring, and capable of accomplishing bigger things. The difference between success or failure in life is having the heart-power to rise from defeat again and again with renewed effort. Tenacity and effort are efficacious human characteristics.

The Bible, a book of unparalleled wisdom, offers an excellent guideline regarding the importance of diligent effort. One of the original rules for successful living that God communicated to man was "Six days a week are for your daily duties and your regular work, but the seventh day is a day of Sabbath rest before the Lord your God."

In an age when man seeks to work less and have more leisure, such a precept might seem outdated to men of contemporary thought. However, to men of wisdom, the implications of this precept are profound and time-less. The wise understand that techniques and methods change, but that principles never do. This premise tran-scends the scope of shallow intellectualism.

God gives man the principle of working "six days a week" because he knows the heart of man explicitly. He knows that man's basic nature is predisposed toward mis-chief and slothfulness. He understands that it is essential for man to develop the character traits that "six days a week" of work will teach him. Responsibility, discipline, perseverance, courage, commitment, confidence, in-tegrity, cooperation, harmony, and purpose are all im-portant attributes gained from useful work. He also knows that "Idleness is the devil's workshop."

Too much leisure is the cause of many troubles for an unprincipled man. Such a man is susceptible to every sort of malady. Habitual gaming, crippling alcoholism, chronic licentiousness, mental disorder, physical disease, criminal acts, and perpetual boredom are common. Leisure be-comes his unequivocal nemesis.

Six days of work and the seventh day for Sabbath rest is a principle that was conceived by Infinite Wisdom for man's own benefit. Starting out in life, a man must invest much time and expend great effort in order to perma-nently chisel his name on the monument of success. "Six days a week," properly organized and planned, are suffi-cient to accomplish this task. The seventh day, the Sabbath rest, must be reserved for spiritual, mental, and physical renewal. It is this ongoing seventh-day renewal that enables a man to be at peak performance during his six days of labor. Both work and renewal are required to achieve a balanced, successful life.

F. Robert Earls chose a career in sales. He was young, educated, talented, and brimming with enthusiasm. His dream was "financial independence by age forty." He threw himself into his work as few men ever do. Twelve-hour days, seven days a week, were common. He was the top salesman of his company month after month. His income soared, but something was secretly happening to him.

Robert discovered himself losing interest in his work. He dreaded getting up in the morning. His zeal for making sales waned. Depression surfaced and, in time, consumed him. Everything he had worked so diligently to achieve suddenly became unimportant. Failure quickly followed. He resigned from his sales position in complete humiliation. Today he works from nine to five in a dead-end job for the federal government. He is bored and dissatisfied. He dreams only of retirement.

Keith W. Pritchard was Robert's best friend. They attended the same high school and were roommates during college. They both chose sales careers, representing the same company. However, this is where the similarities between the two men cease.

When Keith began his sales career, he visualized his new undertaking as a long-term commitment. His company's trainer told him that, on the average, it would require from three to five years to develop a good clientele and reach the level of income that he desired. He believed what he was told and established his goals and plans to best facilitate consistent effort. His aspirations were realistic, yet challenging.

Keith took time to think and plan in detail. Monday through Saturday, he allowed nothing to interfere with his daily plans. Then, on Sunday, he accompanied his family to church, spent quality time with his wife and children, and rested his mind and body. He wasn't aware at the time that his work habits followed a divine precept. He was simply using what he called "common sense."

As the months passed, Keith was consistently among the upper twenty percent of salesmen with his company, but not once was he ever number one like Robert. Also unlike Robert, he devoted almost as much time and effort to servicing clients and cultivating potential clients as he did to selling. Month after month his clientele grew steadily and, consequently, so did his earnings. He stayed right on target to achieve his goals and thus accomplished his purpose.

Keith learned to enjoy his work as he matured, gained experience, and began to taste the fruits of his labor. His job grew into a labor of love. He was deeply saddened when Robert decided to throw in the towel. He had attempted to help his friend, but to no avail. Robert had permitted his attitude to become so negative that he blamed others for his circumstances. He even blamed Keith. Keith discerned that Robert was beyond help.

Today, Keith is well-to-do. His independence allows him to do all the things that he wants to do. He is dedicated to God, family, country, and career. He lives a rewarding life because he invests a significant amount of time helping others, as well as providing for his loved ones. He is a happy and fulfilled person with a bright future.

The lives of these two men are classic examples of the creditability of divine principle. Generally speaking, they had similar backgrounds and attributes. Their aspirations and dreams were similar also. But Keith paced himself by working six days and renewing himself on the seventh, while Robert labored incessantly without the benefit of adequate self-renewal. As a result, Keith's effectiveness increased, while Robert's decreased. He literally burned himself out.

Once Keith became well-established in his business, he found the freedom to organize his daily schedule so that it was less demanding. He planned more efficiently so that he had adequate time to conduct business and yet more time for his family and personal interests. These were privileges that he earned through sustained effort. It should be emphasized that, from the beginning, Keith paid the price of "six days a week" of toil, which prepared him for greater personal freedom.

The experience of a mature, well-established man makes him wise enough to manage his leisure time properly while avoiding the common pitfalls that undermine success. This is certainly the case regarding Keith's situation.

Effort, both mental and physical, makes the seeds of discovery blossom and the wheels of enterprise turn. There is no accomplishment without effort. It is the pillar on which the fortune of humanity rests. There is no substitute for effort in man's ongoing pursuit of progress.

Common sense reveals that the man who invests sixty hours of productive time to his vocation each week will accomplish more than the man who invests forty hours per week. The first invests a minimum of eighty hours more every month, which equates to nine hundred and sixty hours annually. This is the equivalent of having one hundred and twenty additional eight-hour workdays per annum, and six and one-half additional work years over a twenty-year period.

In essence, a twenty-year-old man who works ten hours each day, six days a week, for twenty years, will gain the equivalent of six and one-half years of productive effort over a twenty-year-old who works eight hours per day, five days per week, for the same period of time. The advantage is much the same as having a thirty-meter head start in a one-hundred-meter foot race. Extra effort, plus time, transforms the life of an ordinary man into an extraordinary existence.

The great Solomon wrote, "Lazy people want much but get little, while the diligent are prospering." To lazy people, the prosperity of others is a mystery that they attribute to luck, nepotism, greed, or corruption. They choose not to face the truth: that people rise to fortune in this world by the power of thought and the resulting effort they employ. All honest gain requires mental and physical effort, and the greater the effort, the greater the gain. For certain, the diligent prosper. There is no legitimate exception to this universal truth.

These profound words from the gifted, skillful pen of Henry Wadsworth Longfellow illuminate the blessings of effort:

> The heights by great men reached and kept
> Were not attained by sudden flight,
> But they, while their companions slept,
> Were toiling upward in the night.

Diligence is the child of commitment. In 1623, a diligent pilgrim father named Timothy Ashley conquered the mighty Atlantic in a small sailing vessel to give his family a fresh start in the New World. Their craft touched shore at what is now Bar Harbor, on the rugged Maine coast.

Once they had landed safely and made camp, Ashley took an ax and proceeded to chop his vessel into pieces, which they used for firewood. This brave and calculated act left him and his family with no possible means of retreat. His commitment was then unconditional and complete. They had no other choice except to succeed—and they did!

Carefully choose your labor of love and put all of your heart-power into it, for it will become the access to your dreams, the channel to accomplishing your purpose, the outlet that satisfies the hidden forces at work within, the creativity that provides constant challenges and unlimited potential. Such a commitment cannot and will not be denied fulfillment.

A total commitment to your labor of love will inevitably ensure your success. Consequently, when you one day reach the end of life's road and glance over your shoulder at your footprints through time, you can honestly and proudly say, as did the vigilant Apostle Paul, "I have fought the good fight, I have finished the race, I have kept the faith."

❖ POWER THOUGHT ❖
Concentrated effort is the essential ingredient of a dream fulfilled.

Chapter 4

RESPONSIBILITY

Responsibility walks hand in hand
with capacity and power.
　—J. G. Holland

The success that a man achieves or the failure that he endures is the consequence of his most dominant thoughts. Higher Law, which governs everything that exists, is impartial, immutable, just, and true. In the universal scheme of things, every human being must play out the game of life under the same set of rules, with no one person having an advantage over another. A man must accept the responsibility for his fortune.

A man's thoughts are his creation. Morality and immorality, lawfulness and unlawfulness, happiness and unhappiness, and success and failure are of his choosing. His will defines his environment. He cannot truthfully credit or blame another person or entity with the responsibility for his circumstances. Nor can he delegate the responsibility of changing his environment to another person or entity, for he alone can will it to happen. Everything that a man is, or ever will be, first develops in his mind. There are no means of escaping the effects of this profound reality.

A man may establish a beneficial foundation for responsible living by adopting and following these time-tested rules:

1. I am the Lord your God. You shall worship me only.
2. You shall not create and serve idols in any form.
3. You shall not use my name irreverently.
4. Remember the Sabbath day by keeping it holy.
5. Honor your father and mother.
6. You shall not murder.
7. You shall not commit adultery.
8. You shall not steal.
9. You shall not give false testimony against your neighbor.
10. You shall not desire your neighbor's spouse or possessions.

These inspired precepts are the ten pillars on which Western civilization was built. They also represent foundation stones for millions of people throughout history who have built successful lives. Responsible nations and individuals who build upon these precepts reap bounteous blessings. Experience has proven that each is a potentially rewarding guide by which everyone should strive to live.

A successful man cannot help an unsuccessful man unless the latter chooses to cooperate. Too often, it is only when the latter reaches the end of his rope that he becomes willing to be helped. Even then, the successful man can do no more than counsel, demonstrate, and encourage. The man who fails must assume the responsibility for his failure, garner his courage, and engage a noble purpose if he is ever to rise above his desperate condition. This is something that he alone can do.

Jeremy Q. Lyons was the president of a West Coast company that manufactured a popular brand of typewriters and controlled a major portion of the national marketplace. With the development of word processors and computers, however, the market demand for typewriters dwindled steadily. Lyons, who was known to be unreceptive to change, vowed to continue manufacturing typewriters anyway. Sales plummeted, eventually plunging the company into bankruptcy. Until the bitter end, Lyons believed that the market for typewriters would revive.

Hundreds of employees lost their jobs, including the president, who blamed the computer industry for his misfortune. He resorted to alcohol as the solution to his problems. Numerous job interviews proved unfruitful. Depression overtook him, creating a deeper dependence on the bottle. In time, he lost every possession. His wife reluctantly took their small daughter and moved in with relatives. Lyons found himself on the streets, sleeping at the downtown mission.

One day a friendly businessman saw Lyons sitting on a park bench drinking cheap wine. Lyons was visibly embarrassed. The businessman took an immediate interest in the derelict, visiting him regularly and encouraging him to change his circumstances and rejoin society. His efforts met with minimal results.

Early one morning a policeman found Lyons lying in a pool of his own urine in a gutter behind the mission. There was little life left in him. A crack medical team worked a miracle and gave him a chance at recovery. The physician told him that if he didn't stop drinking alcohol, it would soon kill him. In great despair, Lyons knew he had reached the bottom of the world's garbage pail.

The better part of a week dragged by before the businessman visited Lyons in the hospital. His only friend was quick to discern that he had hit rock bottom. For the first time, he was receptive to help and encouragement.

His friend visited him every day. The two men discussed Lyons's misfortune. Lyons explained how his problems started because of the invention of the computer. Day after day, the friend listened intensely as Lyons painstakingly told how a dreadful series of outer circumstances caused all of his troubles.

Then his friend simply said, "Now that you have experienced the worst that life has to offer, would you like to experience the best that life has to offer?" The question did not surprise Lyons, and he answered with a resounding "Yes."

Numerous visits ensued. His friend recounted Lyons's failure step-by-step, pointing out how the pattern of his thoughts had been the real cause of his problems. For example, he explained that if Lyons's company had converted from typewriter to computer manufacturing in the beginning, it would have seized the opportunity to benefit from the birth of a dynamic new industry instead of participating in the struggle to keep a dying industry alive. Lyons understood and accepted the responsibility for his actions and, consequently, his undesirable circumstances. From that day forward, his outlook changed. He made extraordinary progress in his fight against alcohol addiction.

His friend told him of God's unconditional love. He learned that he is a unique creation, having special characteristics that, when properly employed, would elevate him to achieve his fondest dreams. His friend gave him a Bible and instructed him to read it, emphasizing that the Bible has all of the answers regarding happiness, success, and skillful living. He studied it daily and began to experience remarkable personal growth.

Lyons was astounded by the wisdom that he acquired, especially from the inspired thoughts of the great Solomon. Although excellent schooling had developed his intelligence, no one had ever taught him wisdom. He now saw the shortcomings of his formal education. He began practicing the principles that he learned, and every aspect of his life improved, especially his struggle with alcohol addiction.

Encouraged by his friend, he secured a regional sales position with a national computer company. Because of his background in typewriters, he learned the business quickly. Ironically, he was climbing the ladder of success in the very industry that he had once despised and blamed for his failure.

Lyons's sales results were extraordinary. He even helped a fellow salesman who was failing turn his fortune around. In his thirty-first month as one of the top salesmen in his company, Lyons resigned and opened a computer store. His former employer supplied him with inventory, and he was off and running. During the next sixty months, he opened five additional stores in his market area. His earnings grew well into six figures.

In that same period, Lyons reunited with his wife and daughter and moved into an impressive new home on the eleventh green of a neighborhood country club. He became active in his church, as well as several charitable organizations. He made numerous friends, but never one like the businessman he called "an angel in disguise," who taught him about the power of thought and started him on the road to true success.

Subsequent to getting his life on a positive course, Lyons searched the city for his friend, but there was no trace of him. He checked the city and county tax rolls, voter registration records, and telephone directory. The personnel at the hospital and alcohol rehabilitation center where Lyons had been a patient did not recall ever seeing such a man. His friend had vanished—or possibly never really existed. Could the businessman truly have been an angel in disguise?

In this case, the wrongly directed thoughts of a businessman caused terrible heartache and failure; the rightly directed thoughts of the same man turned his adversity into happiness and success. Once Lyons rightfully accepted the responsibility for his failure, his new perspective enabled him to benefit from his experience. By being honest with himself, he could learn from his past mistakes and build his future on sound principles.

A man remains a slave to outside conditions either through ignorance or by choice. Possibly he might live under the illusion that he is not responsible for his circumstances, a state of mind common to the naive, misinformed, or mislead. Yet, this mind-set is simply mental bondage to ideology, leadership, legacy, or habit. A man living in modern society has no legitimate excuse for not accepting the responsibility for his conditions, even if he is born into them, for the thriving abundance that surrounds him is undeniable evidence of a better way, a way that he has just as much right to walk as any other man. The first step must be responsibility; the second, desire; the third, commitment; the fourth, action; the fifth, patience; the sixth, perseverance; and the succeeding steps are habitual personal growth. Outside conditions cannot enslave the responsible man who discovers "a better way."

Unfortunately, there are rulers and governments that usurp individual responsibility and enslave their populace by oppression, suppression, or dependence on social welfare, which is the opiate of society. These systems of enslavement violate man's God-given rights to liberty and the pursuit of happiness. Such methods of rule will ultimately fail, for the precepts on which they were founded are unsound and, therefore, contrary to Higher Law.

True success cannot bless an irresponsible man who is consumed with the desires of his base nature. Man naturally yields to his animal instincts. He requires no special effort to be evil-minded and to pursue wickedness. Such instincts are present from birth. A child in his initial months of development is not old enough to be substantively influenced by his parents or environment, and yet one of the first words that he speaks is "mine," which reveals the selfish inclination of his base nature. Does he have to be taught to hit other children or to take things that do not belong to him or to disobey his mother? No, for those irresponsible traits are instilled in his heart from the instant life begins in the womb.

To be successful, a man must be responsible and conquer his appetite for baseness and folly, which is ever present within. This is among the greatest challenges of life. A man may be responsible enough to overcome a part of his baseness, yet cling to certain traits that are wretched and still achieve material rewards. This double-minded man is like the waves of the sea blown to and fro by the wind. His thoughts lack power because his mind is unsettled, making concentration difficult, clear thinking improbable, and detailed planning arduous. Because he fails to master his thoughts, he finds responsibilities burdensome and the daily management of his affairs troublesome. His self-imposed limitations are the consequences of his inconsistent thought-life.

A man cannot become responsible, conquer his base nature, and achieve genuine success unless he is willing to make sacrifices. The extent of success that he achieves will be in direct proportion to the extent that he sacrifices baseness and folly, fixing his thoughts on his dream, purpose, goals, plans, and the development of responsible character. The greater his growth and progress, the greater his achievement and lasting success.

Higher Law favors the responsible, the virtuous, the beneficent, the purposeful, the committed, the toiling, the persistent. It is antithetical to irresponsibility, wickedness, avarice, confusion, indifference, slothfulness, and the need of perseverance. Why? Because the Law of Cause and Effect is unfailing.

Arrogance, egotism, and irresponsibility are sometimes the outgrowth of material success, but never true success. An ambitious man rises from scarcity to prosperity. The journey is arduous and long. He then tastes the distinctive flavor of affluence and the power and influence that it wields, tantalizing his base nature. He indulges himself wholly and becomes a glutton at the banquet table of life. Avarice overtakes his soul. He holds others who are not seated at the table in contempt, and is spiteful and envious toward those who are. He imposes his ideals and standards on the simple-minded. To him, perfection is only that which he deems it to be.

Here is a man who gained material success and all of its auxiliary benefits, a commendable accomplishment. Although intelligent, he is irresponsible and unprincipled. His material success created imbalance, malcontentedness, and a distortion of the real purpose of life. He will never attain true success for his thoughts have made him an aberration of Higher Law. Even though he is rich in a material sense, genuine happiness, meaning, and fulfillment shall always elude him. Material success cannot satisfy the inner longings of the human heart to give and receive love or for cheerfulness, substance, and satisfaction. A hollow shell of a person is destined to search for the true essence of life all of his days, seeking but never finding.

True success, where the real essence of life is understood, is the laurel wreath of thought and the prize of effort. Creativity, discipline, and purposeful toil, united through responsible thought, result in a man's ascension to genuine fortune.

When true success is achieved, it must be continuously guarded against the seductiveness of man's base nature, which has an affinity for counterproductive thoughts and actions. Slothfulness, depravity, and lasciviousness are among the worst. These conditions are contrary to responsible living and will bring about a swift decline to failure.

Without question, *true* success is the effect of responsible, concentrated thought. It is the progressive realization of predetermined, worthwhile goals. It is a process that requires balanced living, so that the fullness of life may be experienced. It is a journey into the unknown driven by the power of faith alone.

You cannot ascend to the lofty heights of true success unless you willingly accept the responsibilities commensurate with the measure of your accomplishment. Responsibility educates and refines, which prepares you to assume authority, position, and wealth. Responsible thoughts enkindle responsible acts, which are the stepping stones to great achievement. Sir Winston Churchill said, "Responsibility is the price of greatness." Dream responsibly—think responsibly—act responsibly, and you will ready yourself to handle the many rich rewards that will follow.

❖ POWER THOUGHT ❖

**Personal responsibility begets
healthy self-esteem, stimulates
noble aspirations, arouses resolute
desire, and leads to successful
accomplishment.**

Chapter 5

CIRCUMSTANCES

You think me a child of my circumstances:
I make my circumstance.
  —Ralph Waldo Emerson

A re your present circumstances hold-
ing you captive and keeping you from achieving your
dreams? Insufficient experience, education, training, capital, and opportunity could confine you to a life of unfulfilled potential. If this is true, there is a solution to your
dilemma that will set you free to become the happy and
successful person that you can be.

There are both controllable and uncontrollable circumstances. The first is the type you have the creative
power to determine. The second is the kind over which
you have no creative power, such as acts of God and
events that you had no direct or indirect role in creating.

Controllable circumstances will be addressed here, for
such conditions influence the successful or unsuccessful

outcome of your life. Wisely manage the things that you can control while showing no concern for matters beyond your realm of authority, and you will rise above your undesirable circumstances to achieve your dreams.

The following illustrates both controllable and uncontrollable circumstances with vivid clarity. Search for them as you read the remarkable story of Jerry Chambliss, a man who overcame nearly insurmountable obstacles to create a highly successful sales career.

Jerry was born with a serious kidney ailment that prevented him from participating in the usual activities of youth. Athletic competition was out of the question. All physical exertion was forbidden. He had partial function in just one kidney, and it was gradually failing. He endured one major surgery after another in futile attempts to sustain what function he had. His youth was consumed by his condition.

Upon graduation from high school, Jerry chose to attend college but stopped short of earning a degree. After some deliberation, he decided that he wanted to become an insurance salesman so that he could control his time, providing a situation well-suited to attending to his health problem. In addition, he liked the idea of not having any limits on his earning potential.

The enthusiastic young man compiled a list of insurance agencies from the telephone directory. He began at the top of the list, personally contacting each agency and asking for nothing more than an opportunity to sell and prove himself. He was rejected again and again because of his youth and inexperience. However, he did not give up. He was close to the end of the list when he approached the receptionist of an agency, and before he could utter a word, she looked up at him over her reading glasses and said, "You must be here to interview for the sales position." The quick-thinking young man answered, "Yes, I am." The receptionist immediately introduced him to the sales manager. After an intense interview and detailed testing, the sales manager decided to give him the chance to prove himself. Much to Jerry's delight, the individual for whom the interview had actually been scheduled never showed up. It did not occur to the sales manager just what had taken place.

Jerry was thankful for the opportunity, and he was determined to make the best of it. His enthusiasm was contagious. He threw himself into his work with all the vigor he possessed. Soon he was ranked among the top salesmen in his agency. He finished the next year at the top and almost led the company that his agency represented, a commendable feat that he accomplished the following year. His peers viewed him as one of the best salesmen in his field.

The master salesman heaped year upon year of extraordinary sales results. He was an inspiration to all those with whom he worked. In time, his only functioning kidney deteriorated to the point of failure. Because of his unique condition, he was not an acceptable candidate for transplant surgery. Therefore, his kidneys had to be removed to prevent the possibility of further complications. The surgery was successful, but extremely painful. The recuperation process was also difficult, but Jerry recovered rapidly because of his positive attitude and determination. Soon he was back at selling, reclaiming his role as an industry leader.

A number of years have passed since Jerry began adjusting to living without kidneys. He now must spend three days each week connected to a dialysis machine that cleanses his blood. Consequently, he devotes only three days a week to selling. He keeps his Sundays reserved for mental, physical, and spiritual renewal. His situation has caused him to plan more effectively and work more efficiently. Therefore, his productivity has not diminished, but flourished. Today, he is still considered one of the premiere salesmen in his field.

Here is a prime example of a person who chose not to let the uncontrollable circumstances of poor health and youth deter him from pursuing his dream. Nor did he permit the controllable circumstances of inexperience, the lack of a formal education, and the need for a job thwart his success. In each instance, he consciously overcame his apparent limitations and created new circumstances that were to his own liking. His story is a profound illustration of the power of thought. Jerry steadfastly refused to allow his circumstances to govern his life.

Perhaps your circumstances are imprisoning you in a dungeon of difficulty. Wretched living conditions, unfavorable surroundings, detrimental companions, destructive relationships, inferior education, unsatisfactory employment, chronic slothfulness, inadequate income, low self-esteem, gross immorality, unscrupulous ethics, harmful habits, deficient opportunity, these are all common circumstances that obstruct accomplishment. You can rise above your circumstances just as Jerry Chambliss did. The moment that you make a definite decision to do so, you will set in motion unseen forces that will open the way for you to pass into the realm of your greater destiny. All personal progress begins with a solitary commitment. Without commitment, there can be no sustainable improvement.

In your mind's eye, picture an immense, fertile field. Imagine that you are the farmer who possesses this rich expanse. If your field is sown with good seeds, properly cultivated and tended, it will produce a bountiful harvest. But if you leave this field unattended, all manner of weeds will sprout and grow abundantly. Your fertile field will bring forth a bad harvest just as readily as a good harvest, for by law it must yield whatever roots in the soil in full measure. Therefore, you must be mindful to plant and tend only good seeds if you desire to reap a beneficial harvest. Bad seeds are sown by the four winds and grow without care. Both the good seeds and bad will mature and bear more of their own kind.

The preceding is an excellent illustration of how your mind functions. It, like the field, is very fertile and will grow whatever you plant in abundance. Therefore, you must take care to plant only good thought-seeds. Then you must cultivate and tend the good thought-seeds, keeping your psyche free from unproductive diversions. You must weed out all bad thought-seeds before they take root and grow. Permit only good thought-seeds to occupy your mind, and your harvest will be bountifully rewarding.

Thoughts have power—thoughts create circum-stances—thoughts become things. Every intense thought that is cultivated creates its own distinctive consequences. Your thought-life shapes circumstances, and circum-stances mold destiny. Thus, you alone are responsible for your own success or failure.

Your outer circumstances are but a mirror of your inner perspective. The thoughts that you inwardly hold dear will manifest themselves outwardly. At any particular point in time, the state of your condition is the direct result of your most frequent and intimate thoughts. This explains the meaning of the axiom "As a man thinks in his heart, so is he."

You are where you are today because that is where your thought-life has brought you. The thoughts to which you have given the highest priority have manifested outwardly, bringing you there. Do not attribute your current condition to chance; instead, know that you are where you are by the unerring law of mind. This profound precept is just as applicable to individuals of weak character or chronic failure or disharmonious living as it is to individuals of strong character or perennial success or inner harmony.

As previously discussed, it is true that circumstances created by uncontrollable events are not directly attributable to your thought-life. However, such circumstances are so completely interrelated with your dominant thoughts that they are beneficial to your personal growth. Every experience is an efficacious teacher.

You are a person in process. Throughout your life, you live in a state of continuous change and growth, and in that process, you learn from experience the lessons that life teaches you. The circumstances of your life today will evolve into the new circumstances of tomorrow. Circumstances are ever changing, ever teaching.

You will find the circumstances of your life difficult as long as you permit yourself to be manipulated and directed by outer forces. You must follow the dictates of your heart in relation to sound principle, instead of succumbing to the will of others or the pressure of outside conditions. You will remain in a vacillating, unproductive dilemma until you exercise your will to create the circumstances that you desire and become the designer of your own good fortune.

When you pass from one set of circumstances to another, you will realize that the degree of change that occurs is in direct proportion to your transformed mental state. If you genuinely desire to alter your circumstances in exchange for a richer and more rewarding life, you must progress through a series of changes that will prepare you to attain the realization of a higher existence. Without change, there can be no measurable growth.

You will rise as high as your most esteemed aspirations, descend as low as your most misguided ideas, or fall victim to your most ominous fears. In essence, you will become what you think about. To illustrate that which manifests from the heart, Jesus said, "A good tree cannot bear bad fruit, and a bad tree cannot bear good fruit." He meant that good thoughts do not come forth from a reprobate mind, and bad thoughts do not proceed from a noble mind.

It is impossible for you to fall into contemptible circumstances unless you give rise to them by low-minded thoughts. It is also impossible for you to rise to favorable circumstances unless they are born of high-minded thoughts. Consequently, you are the overlord of your thoughts, the overmaster of your actions, and the overseer of your environment.

From birth, you began the thought process of molding your outer world. During your journey through life, mere wishes, notions, fantasies, and fleeting desires will get you nowhere. But those special dreams that you hold steadfastly in your heart and nurture continuously will, at their appointed time, become reality.

An all-knowing Creator fashioned you to possess the freedom to choose your own destiny. You are just as free to choose failure as you are to choose success, or to choose evil instead of good. The circumstances that surround you are the by-products of your thoughts from the past. Your future circumstances will be the by-products of what you are thinking now.

Thoughts plus actions are the agents of change. Being noble, they emancipate—they redeem—they flourish—they enrich. Being ignoble, they imprison—they dissipate—they diminish—they destroy. Thoughts plus actions are the impetus for either good dreams fulfilled or bad dreams realized. Their result is determined in the mind of the dreamer.

Is it wise for you to spend a lifetime battling to overcome dire circumstances? Such a commitment displays misguided zeal, for you earnestly battle the "effect " while continuing to harbor and cultivate the "cause." Your best efforts will be futile, for through your blindness you will patronize your adversary. To win your battle, you must first attack the cause and eliminate it. Consequently, the effect will be eliminated, changing your dire circumstances. To solve any difficult situation in life, you must deal with the cause, not the effect.

You may wish to improve your circumstances, but at the same time be hesitant to raise your thoughts to a higher realm. Consequently, you will continue in your dilemma. But if you willingly heighten your thoughts, you will discover that your circumstances improve accordingly.

If you want to forsake evil to become good or to rise from poverty to riches, you must make a profound transformation of your thought process, requiring personal commitments and sacrifices. There is a price that must be paid to acquire the things that are worthwhile in life, and the greater the price paid, the greater the reward received.

Cornelius Gentry is an honest, amiable man, but he and his family are poverty-stricken. He wishes for a better life in a more affluent neighborhood, with all the comforts that such affluence would make possible. However, he has never held a steady job. He has been laid off by his employers time and time again. When he finds new work, he doesn't apply himself as he could and feels completely justified in his slothfulness because of the minimal wages that he earns. He is quick to blame the capitalist system for his misfortune.

Here is a man beset with unfavorable circumstances who doesn't understand even the most basic principles of prosperity. In his present state of mind, he will never see his wishes fulfilled. His thought-life is counterproductive. He is his own greatest adversary. He attracts that which he loathes. He will remain impoverished so long as he harbors his slothful, fallacious, feeble thoughts and the actions that follow.

David Levi was a wealthy individual who continuously succumbed to sensual indiscretions, having numerous clandestine liaisons with women who were enamored by his charm and riches. He descended into the depths of infidelity and immorality. Eventually he was consumed by his sexual appetite and began engaging in all manner of perverted practices. His artificial world crashed down on him when he discovered he had become infected with a deadly virus because of his promiscuity. He spent his fortune in search of a miracle cure. A cure he never found. He died a pauper.

Here was a prosperous individual who took good health for granted and ventured into a risky lifestyle that ultimately became his undoing. He sought gratification for his indiscreet tastes, plus the blessing of good health as well. His thoughts and actions were not harmonious. He was either ignorant of or ignored the potential consequences of his misguided thoughts. This man lost his riches, his health, and then his life because he neglected to live by known precepts of prosperity, good health, and morality.

Benjamin Williams became an entrepreneur as a means to get rich. He chose sales as the vehicle he would use to fulfill his dream. He was diligent and learned his craft well. He then began recruiting salesmen who would represent him, expand his marketplace, and increase his sales volume. He was fortunate to acquire a sales force of professionals who were very successful. Consequently, each of their commission earnings soon topped six figures. Williams prospered as his sales force prospered.

Seeing the extraordinary commission earnings of his salesmen, he rationalized that they were overpaid. Therefore, he began to incrementally decrease the percentage of commissions paid to them and kept more for himself. His profits grew prodigiously. However, one by one his successful salesmen found other employment opportunities that did not limit their income potential. His efforts to replace them were futile because the sales opportunities that he then proposed offered no more than average commission earnings. He lost his valuable sales force, but his growing business overhead remained. He alone could not generate enough new sales to meet the financial commitments that he had made when business was booming. He soon grew discouraged and eventually went bankrupt. His dreams of riches were dashed.

Here is an example of a man who created his own grave circumstances, yet blamed others (the salesmen who left him for greater opportunities) for his misfortune. In truth, he was selfish, and his greedy thoughts robbed him of prosperity. He got what he justly deserved. He failed to understand that he alone was the author of his fate.

The preceding examples give testimony to the fact that man, either consciously or unconsciously, is the creator of his circumstances. Each example also illuminates the truth that while some men focus on a noble goal, they knowingly or unknowingly engage in thoughts and actions that are counterproductive and obstruct success.

Search your experience for similar examples of circumstances you have actualized through your own thoughts and actions. Think about each of your personal experiences and glean the important lessons.

Man is such a complex being that it is impossible to interpret his success based solely on the outward circumstances of his life:

- ❖ A man may reveal to the world an appearance of affluence and yet live from hand to mouth.
- ❖ A man may appear to be a pauper and yet possess great wealth.
- ❖ A man may appear to be honest and yet secretly practice dishonesty in some area of his life.

❖ A man may be labeled as dishonest because of his
   visible acts and yet do commendable charitable
   deeds.

The preceding examples discredit the idea that a man
who appears to be wealthy is indeed rich, or that a man
who seems to be poor is in fact poor, or that a man who
projects an honest image is truly what he appears to be,
or that a man who is called dishonest is what he is called
through and through. A man may be one thing in a particular area of his life and yet be another thing in a different area. He may have commendable qualities as well
as despicable attributes. So a successful man of good reputation may bring upon himself the adverse effects of his
secret indiscretions, just as an unsuccessful man having a
disgraceful name may attract the blessings of his most intimate wholesome desires. Each, in kind, is responsible
for his own success or failure, happiness or sadness,
peace or turmoil.

Misfortune is the result (effect) of wrongly directed
thought (cause) in relation to everyday decisions. It is evidence of disharmony within, which is ultimately disclosed without. Although difficult, misfortune contributes
in a positive way to the process of personal growth.

Human experience reveals that a man suffers little, if
any, personal growth when times are good. But let misfortune come, and he will make rapid progress because
of the challenge of overcoming the many pressures that
adversity brings. The good that is reaped from misfortune
is the propensity it demonstrates for the refinement of
character, eliminating traits that are crude, vile, slothful,
hateful, harmful, unproductive, and mentally binding.
Misfortune removes all of the dross, leaving only that
which is valued.

When misfortune strikes, a man should first seek the cause and its remedy. By correcting the cause, he will also initiate forces that will correct the effect, which will be eliminated, resolved, or managed. When the cause of misfortune is resolved, the effect will always come to an acceptable conclusion.

Man does not ascend to the mountaintop of human existence until his inner being and outer being are one in thought, purpose, accomplishment, and spirituality. He then comprehends the nature of genuine success and *true* prosperity. Abundant happiness and good fortune formulate his circumstances. They are his reward for purity of thought.

You will begin your ascent when you accept the responsibility for your circumstances, desist from complaining and blaming others, and probe your mind seeking the concealed thoughts that are the cause of your condition. Once you discover such thoughts, you must eliminate, resolve, or manage them, thus altering the effect that they have on your life.

This discovery should end any penchant you may have for making excuses or for alleging that someone else is responsible for the circumstances of your life. Thus, you will become wise enough to focus all of your mental energy on thinking positive, principled thoughts, using your present circumstances as facilitators of personal growth and achievement.

Knowing these things, you can look back on your past experiences, good or bad, and discern that every situation was the outer manifestation of your inner condition. In effect, your outer existence is shaped by your inner existence. Your thought-life molds your tangible lifestyle. Your thoughts are the fertile fields from which your circumstances grow.

Keep in mind that the Law of Cause and Effect always rewards good for good and evil for evil. Therefore, you should strive to train your mind to think only godly, productive thoughts. The fruits of such thoughts are love, joy, peace, patience, kindness, goodness, faithfulness, gentleness, self-control, and achievement. As your mind transforms itself into a powerhouse for good and, consequently, for success and fulfillment, your external circumstances will compliantly conform, creating total harmony between the inner and outer you. It is then and only then that all your outer circumstances will be pure, abundant, and blessed, just as your inner being is pure, abundant, and blessed. When you aspire to this level of human existence, you will perceive life as God intended, full of richness and meaningfulness.

In a moment of vain imagining, you may deny or ignore the existence of Higher Law, but your opinion does not make its existence any less. Be certain that justice is an unwritten law governing life. You will receive the just rewards of your thoughts and actions in one fashion or another, good or bad. You may be assured that order is a dominant law of existence and, when properly invoked, brings harmony, creativity, and beneficial reward. You may be confident that goodness is a spiritual law of being that fosters love and peace. Thus, all you must do to prove the validity of Higher Law is adhere to its principles, and your thoughts and actions will attract good and compensating circumstances.

If you genuinely desire to change your destiny for the better, then stop thinking negative, destructive thoughts, for such thoughts are sure to have an ill effect on your life. You have the freedom to think as you choose. Therefore, choose to think about positive, constructive things, and you will reshape your circumstances and discover opportunities yet unknown.

Your environment is a mirror that reflects the thoughts that have made you what you are. Take your thoughts to a higher plane, and the image in the mirror will change into a new, superior environment. Fate has not ordained that you must live in lean circumstances. You do so through either ignorance or choice. Your greater destiny beckons. Go now and seize it.

❖ **POWER THOUGHT** ❖

A truly enlightened man uses his circumstances as stepping stones to his greater destiny.

Chapter 6

CHARACTER

The discipline of desire is
the background of character.
—John Locke

The distinctive attributes of a man create the image he projects to the world—an image known as character.

Modern education neglects to impart profound knowledge. This is a colossal mistake. By learning wisdom, students acquire the principles necessary to develop noble character.

Generations of intellectually astute students devoid of wisdom have been graduated into society. As a result, they have resorted to relativism as the guide for their behavior. They were not taught to stand on principle, but to rely on their own instincts as they relate to any given situation. Consequently, we have an emerging populace that has no firm standards and, therefore, that finds

the real issues of life impossible to reckon with successfully.

The incidence of murder, rape, incest, theft, and civil
violence has increased in direct proportion to the decrease of character of our citizenry. Weakness of character among a people is a breeding ground for every kind
of perversion. Hatred, greed, deceit, lying, cheating, self-
interest, and licentiousness abound in a society of declin-
ing character.

The shallowness of a people of low character will
cause them to elect presidents, congressmen, judges, and
other government officials who are of the same persua-
sion. The results are inept government and corruption.
The opinion that an elected official's character isn't important if he can get the job done is a false premise. It is
symptomatic of voters without principle. Character and
acts cannot be separated. An elected official's acts are
merely the visible evidence of his character.

No nation or individual can escape the consequences
of the Law of Cause and Effect. The Law is absolute and
is no respecter of persons. Even Theodore Chadwick
Smith, a rich and powerful corporate executive, is subject
to its indistinguishable authority. The Law prescribes that
for every action there is a compensatory reaction. What is
sown is reaped in its own kind and in full measure.
Principled character reaps noble circumstances. Unprincipled character reaps ignoble circumstances. The outward
condition of a person's life is determined by his inward
condition.

Smith possessed a disposition for prevarication,
machination, and libidinousness while a college student
and then as a professor at a major university. Being

deep-rooted from youth, these character traits accompanied him when he made a transition from the classroom to the business arena. His keen intellect, effervescent personality, and incessant zeal eventually won him the chief executive's office of a major corporation, an international company over which he came to exercise axiomatic control. His leadership was soon characterized by questionable business deals and practices. Serious allegations of moral indiscretion, ethical violations, and corporate corruption were made against him by several of the company's officers. Utilizing a cooperative news media, he simply refuted all such allegations with whatever tactics that were necessary to discredit their sources. The same character traits that had pervaded his earlier years matured into a force powerful enough to protect his position and to destroy anyone in the corporate hierarchy who openly opposed him.

Smith's corporate aspirations soon turned from the presidency to gaining the chairmanship of the board of directors. From the beginning, his efforts to oust the current board chairman were countered by personal attacks on his character and ethical practices. Bona fide evidence surfaced that substantiated his adversaries' reports of marital infidelity and improper corporate behavior, which differed greatly from the virtuous persona that Smith had projected to the public. But his brilliance, charisma, and exuberance again served him well as he effectively used the national news media to deny all allegations made against him. Experience had taught him to obfuscate opposing accusations expediently and decisively.

Politically allegiant directors gave Smith a narrow victory by a six-to-five vote. Thus, he became both president and chairman of the board of directors. His sphere of power and influence was now complete. His extraordinary ability had helped him achieve another milestone in his business career. However, this particular accomplishment was the ultimate milestone, for he now had absolute control of a highly successful international company. He now held the most powerful position in the corporate world.

But Smith's actions as chairman of the board revealed a dramatically different business philosophy than the one he had purported to have while politicking for control. He betrayed the directors who had supported him, broke promises to stockholders, and fired capable company executives and replaced them with hand-picked lackeys. Of course, his actions were consistent with former actions that his supporters among the board of directors had neglected to regard.

Secrecy, cronyism, questionable motives, dishonest methods, poor results, and corporate scandal further defined his years in the seat of power. Eventually, a significantly large group of stockholders won a lawsuit they had filed against him on the grounds of corporate misconduct. Several of his senior officers were named in the lawsuit as well. As part of the legal settlement, each was required to make restitution for several hundred thousand dollars of missing company funds that had mysteriously vanished. Each lost his job. The national news media gave the affair their full attention. Smith's inefficacious leadership brought disaster to both him and his hand-picked executives—disaster so resounding that it echoed throughout the corporate world, resulting in ruined careers and destroyed lives.

Noted corporate analysts openly debated various reasons why the debacle might have happened. Those whose opinions were founded on principle reached wise conclusions. Others blamed circumstances, alleging that the offenders were victims of unfair company politics.

There is an old Jewish proverb that says "A rotting fish always stinks from the head." This is an apt metaphor for rotten leadership. The leader, in this case a rich and powerful corporate executive, must accept the ultimate responsibility for his failure, as well as the failure of those whom he influenced. He is the "head" and therefore the vent hole of the foul smell of spoilage. He is the lone individual who has ultimate authority and, consequently, he must accept ultimate responsibility also. This precept is the foundation of effective leadership.

When the rich and powerful corporate executive physically moved into the quarters of the president and chairman of the board, his old character traits moved in with him, and the ghosts of his controversial past followed him. Character is the handiwork of thoughts and actions. Character is important, for an individual cannot be one person in secret and another person publicly. The secret person within must materialize without, even though it may surface only during unguarded moments. Character influences everything in a person's life: ethics, morals, activities, relationships, and career. Therefore, the circumstances of a person's life are interrelated with character, for both are the creation of thought.

The reason the rich and powerful executive became submerged in a perpetual quagmire of conflict, problems, and turmoil is the unfailing Law of Cause and Effect. His thoughts initiated actions, which resulted in the creation of his circumstances. There is no truer evidence of the character of a man than the circumstances that he creates in his life through the power of thought. He is the maker and molder of his state of affairs. He is the craftsman of his character.

Other than the teachings of Jesus, the most profound precept ever recorded came from the inspired mind of the great Solomon, who wrote, "As a man thinketh in his heart, so is he." This precept is so all-encompassing that it affects every area of a man's life—even the secrets that he conceals from the world. This precept asserts that a man's character and, consequently, his circumstances are the sum and substance of all his thoughts. Experience has proven the veracity of this assertion.

The preceding applies to responsible or irresponsible thoughts, planned or unplanned thoughts, and good or evil thoughts. The fertile soil of the mind nourishes the seed-thoughts planted there until they burst forth and grow into tangible harvests.

> No success or failure,
> Blessedness or wretchedness,
> Happiness or unhappiness,
> Is ever wrought,
> Unless it first becomes a thought.

The outcome of a man's life is determined by his personal growth as it relates to cause and effect. He does not acquire great character by luck or favoritism or the endowment of special genes from birth. Instead, he acquires it as the result of years of deliberate striving and practice to attain noble-minded thought. He cultivates his mind to reject negative thoughts that will retard his personal growth, as he aspires to think positive thoughts of happiness, success, and godliness, which are hallmarks of great character.

The Law of Cause and Effect prescribes that a man is the architect of his own character. Within his mind he designs the thoughts by which his personal image is molded. Through the proper application of thought, he makes wise choices, which are rungs up the ladder to good fortune and, consequently, good character.

Somewhere in between the two extremes of success and failure lie the varying degrees of personal growth. The vast majority of people accept life shaped and molded by their outer circumstances, preventing them from ever discovering the blessedness of high achievement and character development.

Other than a man's discovery of God, there is no greater revelation than learning that he is the lord over his mind, the creator of his character, and the prophet of his own future. Being the lord over his mind, he possesses the potential to change and improve his character at will. This awareness enables him to be whatever he chooses to be.

The Law requires that a man seek within to uncover hidden weakness, secret baseness, and to analyze experience. By exploring the depths of his mind through arduous investigative thought, he discerns the vexing issues within that inhibit his personal growth. Such discovery is essential if he is to correct his course and become all that he is meant to be.

Will Stevens had begun digging holes in search of gold in the Colorado Rockies in 1864. He dreamed of making a strike that would make him rich. Prospecting was hard and lonely work. The winters were long, extremely cold, and logistically difficult. Sometimes the isolation nearly drove him mad.

Stevens made many acquaintances in the gold fields, a number of whom discovered their bonanzas. Two of his closest friends hit it rich in Gilpin County in 1866. He found it deeply discouraging that he had worked harder and longer than any of them, but to no avail. He often considered quitting, but he could never bring himself to do it. His dream would not fade and prevented him from giving up.

Early in 1874, he was digging in California Gulch, finding just enough gold to purchase his meager provisions. A year passed, during which his takings improved, but not significantly.

Stevens's sluicing operation kept getting clogged because of a heavy black sand that made progress almost impossible. A geologist friend of his became curious about the troublesome soil. He took samples and assayed them. The heavy black sand turned out to be carbonate of lead, which had forty ounces of silver to the ton.

Stevens's dream was realized—he hit it rich! History was made, for his find was the beginning of a silver mining boom from which the town of Leadville grew.

This determined man searched tirelessly, enduring much hardship and finding little but rock in the numerous tunnels he dug. However, he never ceased his quest until he discovered the answer for which he searched.

This same principle applies to a man who explores the depths of his mind seeking answers that will change his life for the better. Thinking is hard work. Sometimes it must be done for long periods of time to achieve the desired results. Tunnels of thought must be dug into the psyche to uncover hidden enigmas that obstruct personal growth. A sluicing process must be enacted to eliminate those enigmas. Then the riches may be mined, preserving their value, purity, and beauty. No gold or silver mine ever held as much potential for wealth as a principled mind.

Begin now to analyze the effects of your past thoughts on your present circumstances and character. Trace how they have molded your life and determined your future. Explore how they have affected others. See how they have created the personal image that you project to the world. Discover how they have control over everything from your most frivolous affairs to your most supreme accomplishments. An objective analysis will prove the veracity of the Law. You will find Cause and Effect to be infallible.

Knowing these things, you will fathom the truth and power of Jesus' words "He who seeks finds." You may now be certain that you hold the key that opens the door to your future, for you possess the free will to make choices. Choose to be of noble character, and true success will pervade your circumstances. Heraclitus, a sixth-century Greek philosopher, wrote, "A man's character is his fate"—an immensely profound conclusion.

❖ **POWER THOUGHT** ❖

**Scientific advancement,
technological revolution, and
the expansion of knowledge
can never supplant the need
for character.**

Chapter 7

FAITH

*Faith means belief in something concerning
which doubt is theoretically possible.*
— **William James**

The intellectual and wise Apostle
Paul defined faith in a classic way: "Now faith is being
sure of what we hope for and certain of what we do not
see." The implications of this simple declaration transcend
time and are so comprehensive that they relate to every
part and parcel of life.

Faith is a frequently used and often misunderstood
word in our modern society. One man argues that the secret of success is having faith in yourself. Another advocates that by exercising faith you are God, capable of
unlocking the mysteries of life. Still another insists that the
way to good fortune is to demonstrate faith in your goals.
The opinions about this subject are countless. Although

such opinions offer some measure of reward, they all fail to withstand the tests of time and enduring satisfaction.

The reason such opinions prove imperfect is that they are of finite origins. Man himself is imperfect, and therefore the creations of his mind and the works of his hands are also imperfect.

A very famous attorney violently took his own life. The common question from the lips of the masses was "Why?" To them, he appeared to have everything that a man could want: a lovely family, beautiful home, money, prominence, power—success by the world's standard.

Why did he kill himself? The object of his faith was wrongly focused. Therefore, he became the victim of misplaced faith in someone or something finite. When he realized the imperfection of the object of his faith, disillusionment ensued, disappointment developed. He eventually fell into abysmal depression. Feeling let down, mortified, deflated, and disgraced because of the cracks that he discovered in his icon, he found life hopeless and grew suicidal.

Let his example be a reminder to never make man or position or things the object of your faith, for finite icons with their many imperfections will one day bring you sore disappointment and intense dissatisfaction. This is a lesson that man has learned through much despair and many heartaches.

A wise man willingly places *all* of his faith in the infinite God—the great I AM—the Author of life—the Creator of the universe—the loving Heavenly Father. God is spirit. His presence permeates the cosmos. It lives in the hearts of all men who love him. This indwelling spirit empowers human beings with the potential to develop supernatural faith, a faith that is wisely focused, unshakable, productive, and rewarding.

Faith in the finite has limitations and is no more powerful than the object in which such faith is concentrated. Faith in the infinite has no limitations, and all the power of Heaven upholds it. Man's imperfect character undermines faith in the finite. God's perfect character underpins faith in the infinite.

No man is deserving of the unconditional faith of another because the essence of his character lacks perfection. To the contrary, the infinite God is worthy of a man's unconditional faith because of his preeminent character:

- ❖ He is the *sovereign* of the universe; everything is under his control.
- ❖ He is *righteous*, incapable of any wrongdoing.
- ❖ He is *just*, being completely fair.
- ❖ He is *loving*, giving his love unconditionally.
- ❖ He is *eternal*, having no beginning or end.
- ❖ He is *omniscient*, knowing everything.
- ❖ He is *omnipotent*, wielding unlimited power.
- ❖ He is *omnipresent*, being everywhere in spirit at the same time.
- ❖ He is *immutable*, always the same, never changing.
- ❖ He is *truthful*, forbidding deceitfulness and falsehood.

The man who avidly places all of his faith in the living God will not be disappointed. He is a wise man. King David, the inspired psalmist who through both accomplishment and adversity grew to know his Maker in a most personal way, wrote: "Be delighted with the Lord. Then he will give you all your heart's desires. Commit everything you do to the Lord. Trust him to help you do it, and he will." The king knew from experience that putting complete faith in human beings would invite disappointment and troubles, but that committing his faith to the King of Kings would bring fulfillment and true success.

You have the choice of putting your faith in finite things or in the Infinite Source of man's sustenance. The choice you make is of paramount importance for the former is temporary by nature and without lasting substance, while the latter is permanent and pregnant with rich, enduring rewards. Your thoughts concerning this important choice will establish the pattern for harmony and serenity in your life and determine your destiny. If you are wise, you will choose the latter and experience the best that life has to offer.

When you put faith in God for the successful outcome of your life, He becomes a perfect conduit through which your thoughts are channeled in regard to the formulation of your dreams, purpose, goals, and plans. You will discern God's guidance through the urging of his indwelling spirit and the principles for successful living gleaned from the Sacred Scriptures. The spirit and the Bible are the only two sources of information from which you may discover God's perfect will for your life and how to achieve *true* happiness and success.

You communicate with God through prayer. "Ask, and you will be given what you ask for." Prayer is simply having a mental or verbal conversation with your Heavenly Father, just as you would with a wise and caring earthly father. You are free to discuss anything, or ask anything, knowing that the response you receive will be loving and true, and that his guidance will always be in your best interest. "The earnest prayer of a righteous man has great power and wonderful results." Your omniscient Heavenly Father knows all sides of every question and therefore is capable of discerning perfect answers.

Your genus species is *Homo sapiens,* which means wise man. You are the only creation having the ability to think, reason, create, and choose your own destiny. The fact that you possess intelligence and a free will makes you unique in the animal kingdom. Your Creator deliberately made you so that, as his highest earthly creation, you can fulfill his mandate to be fruitful, multiply, and assume dominion over your material environment. He also gave you the free will to accept or reject him as God. Hence, you must choose the path of your earthly walk, as well as the course of your eternal destiny. The choices are either to make that journey alone or with God as your omniscient guide. This is the most important decision that you will make during your lifetime.

No man is endowed with great faith from birth. Faith is something that grows slowly through continuously increasing knowledge, practice, and experience. Thought, properly focused, helps stimulate this continuing growth.

Moses fled from Egypt in fear for his life. His brothers, the Israelites, were in captivity there. Pharaoh had ordered his arrest and execution. He went into the land of Midian in search of a safe haven and settled there, eventually taking a wife and becoming a shepherd of her father's flocks.

One day while he tended the sheep near Mount Horeb, God spoke to him from the midst of a burning bush. God said, "I am going to send you to Pharaoh, to demand that he let you lead my people out of Egypt." The mere thought of returning to Egypt and facing the king made Moses' blood run cold.

The shepherd covered his face with his hands, for he was afraid to look at God. He meekly answered, "But I'm not the person for a job like that!" His answer revealed that his faith in God and himself was weak.

God replied, "I will certainly be with you." Now you would think that God's support would be all that Moses needed to accept the challenge, but he still questioned God and was consumed by doubt. He made excuses: "They won't believe me! They won't do what I tell them to. They'll say, 'Jehovah never appeared to you!'" God had Moses demonstrate several miracles that he could perform before the Israelites and Pharaoh that would prove he was there by divine decree. He threw his shepherd's staff on the ground, and it turned into a serpent. He picked it up by the tail, and it became a shepherd's staff again. His hand was made white with leprosy and then cured right before his eyes.

Having witnessed these supernatural feats, Moses still wasn't convinced and pleaded, "O Lord, I'm not a good speaker. I never have been, and I'm not now, even after you have spoken to me, for I have a speech impediment."

God answered, "Who makes mouths? Isn't it I, the Lord? Who makes a man so that he can speak or not speak, see or not see, hear or not hear? Now go ahead and do as I tell you, for I will help you to speak well, and I will tell you what to say."

Again you would think Moses would say, "OK, if you're behind me, Lord, I'll do it." But instead, he begged, "Lord, please! Send someone else!" His self-esteem and faith were indeed feeble.

At this point, God became irritated with Moses, but having empathy for him, the Lord chose Aaron to be his personal spokesperson to Pharaoh and the people. Moses then reluctantly accepted the mission of freeing the Israelites from Egyptian bondage.

When Moses told Pharaoh that God had sent him with the message "Let my people go," he met strong opposition. The king made the plight of God's people even more difficult and, consequently, they held Moses responsible.

Moses cried, "Lord, how can you mistreat your people like this?" In essence, God then told Moses to stand aside and observe the effects of divine power. The shepherd showed little faith as circumstances grew more critical.

The Lord unleashed supernatural pressure on Pharaoh and his kingdom. First, Aaron's staff was cast on the floor and turned into a serpent right before the king's eyes. Pharaoh was unmoved and refused to let the Israelites go. Next, Aaron touched the water of the Nile with the staff, and the river turned to blood, killing all the fish. Pharaoh was still unimpressed and would not let the people go. Then God increased the pressure by sending plagues of frogs, lice, flies, disease, boils, hail, locusts, darkness, and the death of all firstborn Egyptian sons. Finally, Pharaoh relented and freed the people of God from their slavery.

During this time of intense supernatural pressure, which literally devastated the land of the Pharaoh, Moses' faith grew exponentially. Why? His knowledge exploded. He took the necessary action to accomplish his purpose. His experience heightened copiously. He was becoming a man of great faith—faith that is capable of moving mountains.

This Moses was not the same Moses who had once cowered before God and said, "Lord, please! Send someone else!" He had changed dramatically. This Moses was a man with a purpose who calmly stood on the shore of the Red Sea as Pharaoh's charioteers threatened to overtake and murder the Israelites. He raised his staff, waved his hand over the waters, and the sea parted, making a dry path for the people of God to pass to the other side.

Pharaoh and his chariots were in hot pursuit and entered the pathway through the sea between the two walls of water. When the last Israelite had safely reached the other side, Moses again raised his staff, waved his hand over the waters, and the sea came together, drowning all of the Egyptians. Because of Moses' faith, God used him to successfully rescue an entire nation of people from the vise-grip of slavery. God works miracles through men of faith who are available and willing.

The growth of Moses' faith did not end on the shore of the Red Sea. His ultimate purpose was to lead the Israelites to their Promised Land. Another forty years passed before he actually laid eyes on that country. During that period, he led the grumbling, rebellious Israelites as they wandered the desert in search of the land that flowed with milk and honey. His faith was tested again and again, sometimes while in the midst of seemingly impossible circumstances, but each test simply made his faith stronger.

On Mount Sinai, in the wilderness, God revealed the Ten Commandments to Moses. He also gave Moses detailed instructions regarding how the Israelites were to be governed and how they should live. The wilderness experience, although extremely difficult, was a period of immense personal growth for Moses.

When in triumph Moses stood on the Pisgah Peak of Mount Nebo and surveyed the Promised Land through aged eyes, he knew that he had achieved his purpose in life. "It is the Promised Land," the Lord told him. Just imagine what he must have felt in his heart. He had accepted the challenge, dedicated himself to his purpose, fought against overwhelming odds, finished the grueling mission, and lived to see his dream fulfilled. Moses achieved greatness because of his great faith. Again, keep in mind that this is the same man who once pleaded, "Lord, please! Send someone else!"

As Moses rose from total obscurity to greatness, he passed through five distinct phases in the building of his faith. These five phases are applicable to you as you ascend the stairway to your dreams. Perhaps you may even relate your current situation to one or more of these phases. Engrave these precepts indelibly in your mind, and you will then understand the importance of precise thought as it relates to the process of building faith that is strong enough to ensure success.

THE IDEA PHASE

Ideas are the seedlings from which great accomplishments grow. But they will die if they are not nurtured by concentrated thought and effort, which gives them form, energy, and substance.

Oliver Wendell Holmes wrote: "Many ideas grow better when transplanted into another mind than in the one where they spring up. That which was a weed in one becomes a flower in the other, and a flower again dwindles down to a mere weed by the same change. Healthy growths may become poisonous by falling upon the wrong mental soil, and what seemed a nightshade in one mind unfolds as a morning glory in the other." Ideas originate from two sources: from the minds of others and through your own creativity. So be receptive to ideas that others bring to you, as well as those you initiate, for who knows for certain which will have the potential for good fortune? Once you discover a special idea that moves you to action, put all of your heart-power behind it.

The idea phase is the formative stage in the process of building stout-hearted faith. It is a time of decision, when you must contemplate both the positive and negative aspects of any idea that you consider. This happened to Moses when God brought him the idea of being the man who would lead the Israelites out of Egyptian bondage.

Moses had very little information on which to base a decision. There was no precedent regarding the challenge before him. Therefore, he had no facts that he could consider. He was consumed by doubt and paralyzed by fear. He made excuses and seethed with frustration.

Yet, God insisted that Moses could meet the challenge and persisted in applying maximum pressure, all the while assuring him of divine support. Moses vacillated. He begged. God simply kept on challenging and assuring him that he was the right man for the task. Finally, the shepherd conjured up just enough faith to feebly accept the idea. At that point, he successfully passed through the idea phase and entered the next phase.

You too may find the way difficult when you are faced with an idea that is both challenging and potentially rewarding and that requires a demanding decision. Know that you are simply in the idea phase of building your faith to meet the proposed challenge. Gather and consider all facts if they are available. Seek the wise counsel of two or three individuals who are knowledgeable, experienced, and successful with regard to the idea. Give it much concentrated thought. Pray about it, constantly asking God for guidance. Once your way becomes clear, conjure up just enough faith to either accept or reject the idea. If you accept it, you are ready to pass on to the next phase of building your faith. If you reject it, you must then begin screening other ideas in search of that special one that is ideal for you.

THE TESTING PHASE

Once you seize a noble idea and undertake the quest of bringing it to fruition, you may be certain that your resolve will be tested. In fact, it may be tested numerous times.

After Moses accepted the idea of going to Egypt to free the Israelites, his faith began being tested in various ways. When he first stood before Pharaoh and demanded that God's people be set free, the ruler laughed in his face and responded by increasing the persecution of the Israelites. Twelve more times he repeated the demand to Pharaoh and was rejected. The king tested Moses' conviction to the maximum degree.

Moses observed how completely God supported him, even to the extent of providing miracles. His faith grew stronger each time that he withstood a test. Consequently, the shallow faith that urged him to go to Egypt matured into a deep faith of uncompromising commitment. The tests that he endured because of the stubbornness of Pharaoh prepared him to encounter the tremendous challenges that were still to come.

When you face difficult tests, rely on the Infinite as your source of strength, and you will stay the course and succeed just as Moses did. A worthwhile ideal is attained by having the courage to withstand and overcome testing. Be prepared to face testing, and you will conquer it when it challenges you. The only obstacles that stand between you and the realization of your dreams are tests of your commitment.

You will discover that, in the divine scheme of things, tests of faith are placed in the way of achievement in order to eliminate the weak-willed who are not genuinely committed to the task. It is truly the stout-hearted who justly succeed. By withstanding each test that you encounter, you will deem yourself ready to enter the next phase of faith development.

THE EMPOWERMENT PHASE

Once you undergo formidable testing and are triumphant, your experience will empower you to assume new heights of accomplishment. Having weathered the storms of initial testing, your commitment to achieve your purpose is unqualified. A total commitment!

When Pharaoh, under intense divine pressure, summoned Moses and said, "Leave us; please go away, all of you," Moses instinctively sensed victory and put aside any remaining doubt he may have had. His confidence soared. He was empowered to meet his future challenges head on.

After four hundred and thirty years of captivity, Pharaoh let the people go. With Moses as their leader, God guided them into the wilderness of the Red Sea. Six hundred thousand men, plus women and children, made the exodus from Egypt. Pharaoh soon had second thoughts concerning his decision to grant freedom to his slaves and decided to give chase and again take them captive. He assembled his chariot corps and pursued the people of Israel into the wilderness.

Now Moses had an entirely new array of challenges. Logistically speaking, there had to be enough food and water to feed the multitude each day. When the people heard the news that they were being pursued by Pharaoh's army, they berated their leader. The charioteers trapped them with their backs to the sea, having no way out of their dangerous predicament. The people were hungry, thirsty, tired, and frightened. They felt that their end had surely come.

However, the empowered Moses said to them, "Don't be afraid. Just stand where you are and watch, and you will see the wonderful way the Lord will rescue you today. The Egyptians you are looking at—you will never see them again. The Lord will fight for you, and you won't need to lift a finger."

Moses' faith had grown to such a degree that he was empowered with complete trust that God would meet their needs, and that his purpose would be achieved. It was then, exercising absolute faith, that he waved his staff over the waters and they parted, opening a pathway to life for the Israelites and a road to destruction for the Egyptians.

Having faced testing and prevailed, you will become empowered by your maturing faith just as Moses was. Consequently, you must willingly invest *all* of your resources—thought, time, effort, money, prayer—toward achieving your purpose. Because of your all-encompassing commitment, you too will be empowered to face every challenge that you encounter, to raise your staff and make a clear pathway through to the other side. Being sufficiently empowered, you will be prepared to pass into the next phase of building faith.

THE PATIENCE PHASE

At this stage of your growth, you must learn that patience is a virtue of true success, for it takes time for the fruits of your effort to materialize. Often empowerment causes impatience. It must be tempered by wisdom and self-control.

After the Red Sea experience, Moses and the Israelites went to Marah in the wilderness Shur, where they found the water bitter and unfit for drinking. Immediately, the people again turned against Moses, blaming him for their difficulty. This is a vivid example of how the masses think. They seldom subscribe to principle and instead follow their herd instincts, reacting like cattle. Keep in mind the numerous miracles they had already seen God perform on their behalf. Still, God loved them and met their need. How? Moses prayed, and the Lord showed him how to make the water sweet. They traveled from Marah to Elim, where they found twelve springs and palm trees, an oasis in the desert.

Moses led the Israelites from Elim into the wilderness of Sihn, toward Mount Sinai. The people continued to complain about their leader and wished that they had never left Egypt. Again, this is an excellent example of mass rationale. They quickly forgot the pain of their former persecution and how God had faithfully met their needs. They also lost sight of their purpose: finding the Promised Land.

Their only concern was their immediate situation of hunger. So God miraculously rained down food from Heaven each day: bread in the morning and meat in the evening. In the evening, great numbers of quail flew into their camp, and the next morning a dew fell, leaving small flakes on the ground. The people ate and were filled. The Lord fed them manna one day at a time, faithfully meeting their needs. But the people still complained.

The Israelites moved onward and made camp at the bottom of Mount Sinai. It was there that God gave them the Ten Commandments, as well as other laws, in order that they could live orderly, rewarding, godly lives. At the time, they unanimously agreed to live by these laws.

God summoned Moses to the mountain to receive the Commandments, which he had written on tablets of stone. The cloud of the Lord covered the mountain, and his presence at the top resembled a fiery inferno. Moses stayed there forty days and forty nights. While their leader was away, the people made an idol of gold and worshipped it. They partied and did immoral things. This is another explicit example of the weakness of human nature when influenced by peer pressure. Although they had just agreed to follow God's laws, without the presence of their leader they resorted to the lusts of their basic instincts.

After Moses came down from the mountain, he became angry at what they had done. He disciplined them and restored order. He then returned to the Lord, asked forgiveness for the Israelites, and pleaded that they not be destroyed because of their gross transgressions. In his mercy, God honored Moses' request, but with one stipulation: there would be punishment. A plague came upon the people—a vivid example of cause and effect.

God also refocused Moses' attention on his purpose: leading the people to the Promised Land. All told, Moses wandered the deserts with the undisciplined Israelites for forty years. An entire new generation emerged during that period. This was the generation that God would permit to enter the Promised Land, a new generation unburdened by the mistakes of its fathers.

The major points relating to the forty-year wilderness journey are clear:

1. The exodus generation never lived to fulfill its purpose because of its defiant attitude and absence of faith.
2. Others, in this case the children of the exodus generation, gained the rewards that their predecessors would have received.
3. Moses' faith remained strong, even during the most onerous circumstances, and focused on his purpose.
4. Although Moses' patience was put to the test again and again, not once did he consider giving up— his patience sustained him.

In your journey through the wilderness of life, you too must exercise adequate patience to give your purpose time to materialize. However, this does not mean that you simply sit under a kumquat tree and wait. To the contrary, you must apply your mental and physical energy to the maximum degree while you "wait." You must remain focused and exert undying faith while you "wait." You must make haste while you "wait." You must live each day as though the reward that you "wait" for lies just over the horizon.

If you keep doing the things that are necessary to achieve your purpose while exercising patience, your reward will come to you just as surely as the sun rises in the east. Patience will sustain you until you progress to the last phase of building faith.

THE REWARD PHASE

Now that you have read about the first four phases of building faith great enough to achieve your purpose, your increased understanding has prepared you to learn of your reward—a reward for your persistent faith.

God eventually guided Moses and the Israelites to the plains of Moab. There they saw Mount Nebo towering majestically on the horizon. Those last hours in which Moses led the people across the burning sands toward the mountain seemed like a lifetime to him. Finally reaching the mountain's base, he left the people there and climbed to the top of Pisgah Peak. The panoramic view that he saw caused him to fall on his knees in thankfulness. "'It is the Promised Land,' the Lord told Moses."

As the great leader's eyes looked across the Jordan River into the land that flowed with milk and honey, he was deeply moved. Tears of joy cascaded down his cheeks and dropped on the rocky mountain peak. He felt an indescribable sense of fulfillment. He had achieved the purpose that God had called him to achieve. With God's guidance, he led the people through seemingly impossible circumstances to the land that the Lord had prepared for them. The faith of Moses had made the impossible possible. The former whimpering weakling ultimately became a leader of Herculean strength because the object of his faith was true, making it possible for him to withstand every trial and thus to increase his faith immeasurably. After forty years of growing commitment, Moses received his reward—a reward so bounteous that it made him one of the principal figures of history.

If you will remain steadfast, you, like Moses, will one day see the reward for your faith, the reward of dreams realized, the fulfillment of your heart's desire.

Many men, having enthusiasm and good intentions, set out to achieve highly in life. But the majority give up their dreams when they are faced with the "testing" or "patience" phase of building their faith. They see obstacles as insurmountable because they fail to keep their eyes focused on the object of their faith. Therefore, they quit trying, and quitting often becomes a habit that follows them throughout their lives.

The following is an excellent example of the challenge of keeping faith precisely focused.

Night fell, and out on the lake the disciples were in trouble. For the wind had risen, and they were fighting heavy seas. About four o'clock in the morning, Jesus came to them walking on the water! They screamed in terror, for they thought he was a ghost.

But Jesus immediately spoke to them, reassuring them. "Don't be afraid!" he said.

Then Peter called to him: "Sir, if it is really you, tell me to come over to you, walking on the water."

"All right," the Lord said, "come along!"

So Peter went over the side of the boat and walked on the water toward Jesus. But when he looked around at the high waves, he was terrified and began to sink. "Save me, Lord!" he shouted.

Instantly Jesus reached out his hand and rescued him. "O man of little faith," Jesus said. "Why did you doubt me?"

The preceding is a classic illustration of the power of faith. When Peter saw Jesus coming toward the boat walking on the water, he conceived the idea of walking on the water also. So he asked, and without any hesitation Jesus told Peter to come to him.

The big fisherman crawled over the side of the boat while keeping his eyes on the Godman who stood on the water with his hands outstretched. As Peter took his first step, and a second, then several more, his focus was on the object of his faith. He actually walked on the surface of the Sea of Galilee just like Jesus.

However, he momentarily allowed his thoughts to wander and quickly glanced down at the heaving waves lapping up on his legs. Suddenly, he doubted his adequacy to do what he was already doing successfully and subsequently became frightened and began to sink. His pivotal mistake occurred when he took his eyes off the object of his faith.

Becoming even more panicked as his head threatened to submerge under the turbulent waters, Peter refocused on the object of his faith and cried out to him for assistance. Jesus bent down, took hold of Peter's arm, and calmly rescued him. As he carried Peter back to the boat, he asked, "O man of little faith, why did you doubt me?" Loss of concentration and doubt caused Peter's failure.

Be sure that you are focused before you step out of the boat on the sea of life in quest of your dreams. Then step out on top of the waves having complete confidence that you will arrive at your destination if you just keep moving and remain fixed on the object of your faith. Jesus did not let Peter drown even though the disciple failed. He immediately came to his rescue, and he will do the same for you, again and again, if you but make him the object of your faith, which will lead to the realization of your purpose. With him as your guide, the possibilities that lie before you are limitless, and your rewards will be everlasting.

❖ POWER THOUGHT ❖
Faith is that which remains after all else is lost.

BALANCE

*There is a time for everything, and a season
for every activity under Heaven.*
— Ecclesiastes 3:1

The dreamer who only dreams never acts. A man bewitched by his purpose loses his perspective. The man obsessed with his work invites maladies. A man overwhelmed by responsibility becomes debilitated. The man immersed in his circumstances lacks vision. A man preoccupied with character exhibits conceit. The man of fanatical faith is imprudent. True success shuns the propensity of man for radical behavior and instead advocates balanced living.

The dreamer must act. He must view his purpose, work, responsibility, circumstances, character, and faith with the proper attitude. He must have a presence of mind identifiable by poise, consistency, prudence, and discernment, a state in which balance assumes highest priority, eliminating fanatical conduct. Thus, dreams fulfilled bear such blessings as meaning, cherishing, respect, gratitude, growth, esteem, tranquillity, and achievement.

There is adequate time to do everything that is worthwhile in life if the days are wisely prescribed, planned, and if your tasks are acted upon at the proper moment. A wise man controls his time judiciously; he does not invest an hour without receiving genuine value for it. He observes the passing of time with as much regret as the outlay of his money. He does not allow a single day to pass without increasing his treasure of virtue, knowledge, and wealth. The literary genius Johann Wolfgang von Goethe wrote, "We always have time enough, if we will but use it aright."

A balanced allocation of time toward perfecting the secrets of great achievement is essential to true success. Emphasis must be placed on the development of the total being. Anything less constitutes imbalance, which is the catalyst for fanatic inclinations. Time thoughtfully allocated to areas critical to personal growth is time wisely invested—time that will bear rich rewards.

TIME TO DREAM

Serious dreamers, those who are the real patrons of mankind, designate specific intervals of quality time during which they regularly engage in creative thought. They are not necessarily more intelligent or talented than others, but they have discovered how to use their minds to call into existence substantive ideas that mature into important works. Only a handful of human beings are capable of this because of the masses' preoccupation with the routine daily affairs of ordinary existence.

Constructive dreams evolve into precise, purposeful ideas that transform into specific goals and definite plans. In the most simple and general sense, dreams become goals and plans in four major areas of life: spiritual, financial, educational, and recreational. Within the scope of these four categories, all of the worthwhile activities necessary for skillful, productive, enjoyable living may be addressed.

Spiritual Dreams

Man is a spiritual being. He possesses an innate awareness of divine presence. He has an inherent desire to worship his Creator. This consciousness is permanently instilled in his heart. Even natives discovered in remote jungles at the furthermost reaches of the earth, having no prior contact with the outside world, were found to have deep spiritual beliefs. God reveals his presence to every man through his creation. Life, nature, and the heavens are all his unique handiwork.

No man finds genuine fulfillment until he becomes one with his Maker. He will waste his life in search of meaning that satisfies his spiritual yearning until he comes to grips with the reality of the existence of an almighty, personal God to whom he may bond through a simple act of faith. This bonding makes him spiritually whole and resolves the disruptive longing within, for it brings what he so earnestly sought. The rewards of his faith are peace of mind, personal assurance, self-fulfillment, authentic joy, everlasting hope, and eternal security.

The ultimate system of rule governing the universe is Spiritual Law. It is not found in the text of law books, nor can it be detected through the five senses, but it exists just as the law of gravity exists. Evidence of its presence is everywhere. It prevails over natural law and human law, similar to the way an umbrella covers everything under its expanse. Unlike natural and human law, it cannot be machinated by man. It is eternal—having no beginning or end. It is perfect—being changeless and unfailing.

Noble dreams of a spiritual nature beget definitive, principled goals and plans that conform to divine will and ensure the highest degree of accomplishment and fulfillment. This is why the seasoned and enlightened King David proclaimed, "The fool says in his heart, 'There is no God.'" He had experienced spiritual darkness caused by his profane ventures outside of God's will, which took him into the depths of personal anguish and despair. Although he was immensely rich and powerful, he learned the hard way that life's greatest treasure is found in the spiritual realm. The spiritual man gains everlasting rewards of the heart: love, peace, forgiveness, acceptance, completion, and hope.

Financial Dreams

No man justly gains financial independence without first envisioning it in his dreams. If he doesn't dream about it, he cannot achieve it. Dreams create desire, and desire ignites action, and action brings financial rewards.

In today's society, money is such an important factor in the business of living that it affects every area of life. In the spiritual realm, money is required to support churches, compensate clergymen, sponsor ministries, and provide charity. Educational costs are significant and must be provided for adequately. All forms of family and personal recreation require ongoing funding. In essence, the business of living fruitfully requires large amounts of money over the span of a lifetime—money that must be justifiably earned.

Financial dreams should address such items as career, earnings, savings, investments, giving, education, recreation, and personal and household expenses. Financial matters should be effectively managed through a budgeting process that wisely takes even the smallest details into account.

Money is neither inherently good or evil. It is simply a medium of exchange. Man determines to what purposes it shall be employed. Money rightly employed is the root of good. Wrongly employed, it is the root of evil. The heart of man is responsible for the consequences of riches.

Worthy financial dreams stimulate the formation of specific goals and definite plans that, when followed, lead to legitimate financial independence. They create sufficient capital to provide for every contingency of life, as well as money enough to enjoy some of life's pleasures and wealth adequate to live a balanced existence.

Educational Dreams

Knowledge expanded more during the twentieth century than during all of prior history. There appears to be no limits to man's ingenuity—no boundaries regarding his potential to create and innovate. He has fashioned a world in which knowledge is requisite to success.

Knowledge is not an end in itself, but the means to an end. Neither is knowledge power. However, it does hold the potential for power. Knowledge must be acted upon before it serves a beneficial purpose.

In essence, there are two kinds of knowledge: general and specialized. General knowledge is broad-based, in which a person knows a little about a lot. Such knowledge facilitates social grace, awareness, orientation, and vision, but by nature is shallow. Specialized knowledge is focused, in which a person knows a lot about a little. It is essential to personal and career growth and, consequently, to success. Therefore, it must be given highest priority. The proper balance between general and specialized knowledge nourishes a well-developed persona.

In this modern age, education must be a continuing process. Otherwise, obsolescence will subtly triumph. Therefore, specific goals and definite plans must be established that make way for a lifetime of educational growth for every family member. Today, continuing education is not an option, but a necessity in order to live a productive life.

Recreational Dreams

The man who foolishly burns the candle at both ends all his days invites adversity. Disabling illness, broken relationships, habitual dissipation, or unfulfilled living become his fate. What does a man actually accomplish if he conquers the world but loses himself in the process? He accomplishes nothing of imperishable value and yet pays a great price for his misguided fanaticism. Such behavior is destructive and indefensible.

Recreational dreams are equally as important as financial and educational dreams. It is imperative that a man engaged in the long-term pursuit of success establish specific goals and definite plans for the physical and mental care and renewal of his being. Otherwise he will become the victim of his own fallacious zeal.

Both personal and family recreation must be considered. Quality time should be planned to pursue personal recreational interests, as well as family recreational activities. Recreation should be organized to benefit both the mental and physical realms of living. Time wisely devoted to beneficial recreation is time effectively spent; it brings a greater sense of well-being.

If a man is not engaged in the pursuit of his dreams in the preceding four major areas of life, perhaps he should be asleep. This statement is exemplary of the all-encompassing nature of the goal-setting and planning process, which should involve every important function of living. Anything a person might do outside the scope of the four major areas would more than likely be unethical or immoral. Thus, it is far better to be asleep than to take part in degrading activities that undermine noble purpose.

A man who dares to envision big dreams and aspire to their accomplishment must conscientiously strive to maintain balance between his natural attributes and the principal categories of his existence. Balanced dreaming creates fertile seed-thoughts, which grow and mature into true success.

TIME FOR PURPOSE

An honorable dream must be transformed into a well-defined purpose before it can materialize into reality. That purpose must be compelling, it must complement balanced living, and it must embrace comprehensive goal setting and planning in the four major areas of life.

A soul-stirring purpose is so powerful that it can have detrimental effects if it fails to synergize properly with the far-reaching composition of balance. To the contrary, the omnipotent power of a consuming purpose can be the impetus for great achievement if it is kept in perspective regarding a balanced lifestyle. A man's purpose must be defined within the limits of his objectives if he is to live fully and completely.

A well-defined, compelling purpose becomes the wellspring of boundless energy, undying motivation, and perpetual endurance. It is of paramount importance to take time to describe a definitive purpose in writing, a process of literalizing the imaginary. Writing it down requires concentrated mental effort to think it through in detail and to make it complement the spiritual, financial, educational, and recreational areas of life.

TIME FOR EFFORT

Mental and physical effort are God's medicine. They rid man of three unspeakable evils: excuses, folly, and poverty. The greatest genius is the willingness and skill to do a life's work well. There can be no true success without the impelling force of sustained effort.

Ample time must be allotted for productive work in order to ensure the fulfillment of definite plans that bring specific goals to fruition. Effort energetically expended in the four major areas of life assures balanced, rewarding results that bear abundant happiness, satisfaction, and prosperity. Effort is essential to the development of the total man—the importance of which cannot be overemphasized.

TIME FOR RESPONSIBILITY

Much unhappiness and bitterness are spared the man who thinks about what he owes to others rather than what others owe to him. That man fully understands his responsibility to his fellow man, as well as the potential of the unerring principle of doing for others what he would have them do for him. Such a man is wise and will reap many bountiful rewards.

Responsibility distinguishes between right and wrong. It is nourished by principle. It seeks virtue. It is the forerunner of capacity, power, and achievement. It exists only in the world of reality.

The reality of responsibility touches every facet of living among individuals destined for leadership and position. It weighs heavily in the formation of purpose, goals, and plans in relation to the accomplishment of dreams. Responsibility accepts its just role in spiritual, financial, educational, and recreational matters necessary to living an orderly, balanced existence. It is the gatekeeper of thought regarding the real priorities of life.

TIME FOR CIRCUMSTANCES

Present circumstances are the foundational pillars on which the future must be built. They serve as an accurate compass, revealing an individual's immediate situation and exact position for determining a new and superior path in life. They are a launching pad from which an individual may soar to great heights of true success.

A man must face his present circumstances squarely if he is to rise above them in quest of the realization of his full potential. They should be boldly explored, which requires a deep penetration of the inner recesses of one's mind. Once they are acknowledged and their cause is determined, they must be resolved. A new direction must be chosen, leading to an abundant life.

Circumstances do not make the man—man makes the circumstances. To progress, he must create new circumstances that are harmonious with attaining true success— circumstances that support the fulfillment of his spiritual, financial, educational, and recreational objectives. Thus, he chooses to travel the high road of life, which points to contentment and everlasting rewards.

Time for Character

A tree falls in the direction it leans, and it lies where it falls. The underlying precept here is analogous with the character of a man. He goes in the direction he leans, and there he remains. Thus, he should ask himself, "What is the primary inclination of my life? Does it, with its many desires, lean toward good character?" An honest answer is essential to inspired self-improvement.

Character represents the sum of a man's being. Therefore, he must examine himself from a total-person perspective—delving into the spiritual, financial, educational, and recreational realms of existence—if he truly desires to tap his full potential. His dreams must be noble, his purpose pure, his goals and plans ethical. Consequently, there will be no time nor capacity for evil, vile ideas and acts, for he will be completely occupied with balanced personal growth. Character in balance projects an image of wisdom, competence, resolve, order, industry, vision, and virtue to the world—an image that is characteristic of true success.

Time for Faith

Contrary to some schools of thought, God does exist, there are absolutes regarding right and wrong, and man must face an everlasting spiritual destiny. There is more historical evidence confirming these points than any other aspect of history. The man who approaches the archival record objectively will find overwhelming proof of divine existence and authority. And the man who discovers this truth and then believes it can experience a spiritual relationship with his Maker. This is the only completely reliable means of personally validating divine truth. Access into the spiritual dimension of life cannot be accomplished through anything that a man does, such as being godly or giving to charity or doing good deeds—it can only be entered by faith. Faith is what links and permanently bonds a man with God.

A man of genuine faith has infinite resources that he may tap to benefit his spiritual, financial, educational, and recreational practices. Balance is congruous with divine order. This is both a blessing and an advantage in the human arena. Those without faith must depend solely on their human resources and therefore have finite limitations. Faith in infinite resources, however, instills a person with the potential power to accomplish any dream that is worthy of divine blessing. Faith's rewards are confidence, courage, patience, peace, and perseverance. Faith that is focused on God as the resource for true success is faith that will not be denied fulfillment.

In a letter to his nephew Peter Carr, Thomas Jefferson wrote: "If you find reason to believe there is a God, a consciousness that you are acting under his eye, and that he approves you, will be a vast additional incitement; if that there be a future state, the hope of a happy existence in that increases the appetite to deserve it; if that Jesus was also a God, you will be comforted by a belief of his aid and love." The man who lays aside all bias and objectively examines both sides of the issue can come to no other logical conclusion than that God exists. Thus, he has legitimate reason to become a man of faith.

True success can best be defined as skillful, balanced living. It requires putting proper emphasis on all of the important details of life instead of on just one inordinate obsession. Dreams, purpose, effort, responsibility, circumstances, character, and faith—these all come into play when building the spiritual, financial, educational, and recreational areas of existence. They must be acted on through specific goals and detailed plans. They must be fulfilled based on principle.

The rewards of true success are boundless. Among them, happiness, meaning, respect, recognition, progress, fulfillment, prosperity, and spirituality loom foremost. True success is a life lived abundantly.

The power of thought is your most important natural asset. Rightly focused, it will guide you to true success. Wrongly focused, it will steer you along the rocky road to failure. You have the freedom to choose how you will focus the power of thought in your life—so choose wisely because your destiny hangs in the balance.

PART II

CLASSIC
QUOTATIONS

Chapter 9

THE POWER OF WORDS

It is a wondrous thing to tap the psyche of great achievers to gain deeper insight into the secrets of their success. These quotations from their fertile minds reveal many of their most profound thoughts, thoughts that elevate them to lofty heights of accomplishment, wise thoughts that are mysteriously obscure to most.

Sir Winston Churchill wrote, "It is a good thing for an uneducated man to read books of quotations. The quotations, when engraved upon the memory, give you good thoughts. They also make you anxious to read the authors and look for more." The principles gleaned from such classic quotations are enlightening and powerful. The following examples illuminate these points:

"Chance favors the prepared mind."
—*Louis Pasteur*

"Work joyfully and peacefully, knowing that right thoughts and right efforts will inevitably bring about right results."
—*James Allen*

Commit the following quotations to memory so that they may compel you to achieve your greater destiny. Utilize the distilled thoughts of the master achievers to reinforce your private thought-life. It is indeed a wise person who learns to capitalize on the positive thoughts of other successful people. Therefore, enjoy yourself as you journey through the world of classic quotations ahead.

DREAMS

Where there is no vision, the people perish.
—*The Bible, Proverbs 29:18*

Goals are dreams with feet on them.
—*Dexter Yager*

Nothing is so easy to fake as the inner vision.
—*Robertson Davies*

I just want to do God's will. And He's allowed me to
go up to the mountain. And I've looked over, and I've
seen the Promised Land.
—*Martin Luther King Jr.*

You see things, and you say, "Why?" But I dream
things that never were, and I say, "Why not?"
—*George Bernard Shaw*

Reverie is not a mind vacuum. It is rather the gift of an
hour which knows the plenitude of the soul.
—*Gaston Bachelard*

America has been a land of dreams, a land where the
aspirations of people from countries cluttered with rich,
cumbersome, aristocratic, ideological pasts can reach
for what once seemed unattainable. Here they have
tried to make dreams come true.
—*Daniel J. Boorstin*

His life was a sort of dream, as are most lives with the
mainspring left out.
—*F. Scott Fitzgerald*

Dreams come true; without that possibility, nature would not incite us to have them.
  —*John Updike*

Nothing so much convinces me of the boundlessness of the human mind as its operations in dreaming.
  —*Joseph Clulow*

Everything is first worked out in the unseen ideal realm before it appears in tangible form.
  —*Dr. Venice Bloodworth*

Dream lofty dreams, and as you dream, so shall you become.
  —*James Allen*

The mind is the supreme, originating, constructive force in all human endeavor.
  —*Alfred Armand Montapert*

Nothing at last is sacred but the integrity of our own mind.
  —*Ralph Waldo Emerson*

Vision is the art of seeing things invisible.
  —*Jonathan Swift*

Dreams grow holy put into action.
 —*Adalaide Ann Procter*

Foolish men have foolish dreams.
 —*W.G. Benham*

Back of the job the dreamer
who's making the dream come true.
 —*Berton Braley*

All men of action are dreamers.
 —*James Huneker*

Great thoughts reduced to practice become great acts.
 —*William Hazlitt*

And what they dare to dream of, dare to do.
 —*J.R. Lowell*

Beware when the great God lets loose a thinker on
this planet.
 —*Ralph Waldo Emerson*

Thinking is the hardest work there is, which is the
probable reason why so few engage in it.
 —*Henry Ford*

Thinking is the talking of the soul with itself.
—*Plato*

Nurture your mind with great thoughts; to believe in the heroic makes heroes.
—*Benjamin Disraeli*

The universe is one of God's thoughts.
—*Johann Friedrich von Schiller*

Thinking is essentially purposive, directed, and controlled by the conscious exercise of will, and set in motion by the existence of a problem demanding solution.
—*R.W. Jepson*

Spiritual force is stronger than material; thoughts rule the world.
—*Ralph Waldo Emerson*

I like the dreams of the future better than the history of the past.
—*Thomas Jefferson*

I have learned this at least by experiment: that if one advances confidently in the direction of his dreams, and endeavors to live the life which he has imagined, he will meet with success unexpected in common hours.
  —*Henry David Thoreau*

He's a man out there in the blue, ridin' on a smile and a shoeshine . . . a salesman has got to dream, boys.
  —*Arthur Miller*

It is difficult to say what is impossible, for the dream of yesterday is the hope of today and the reality of tomorrow.
  —*Robert H. Goddard*

Thought takes man out of servitude, into freedom.
  —*Henry Wadsworth Longfellow*

Ideas are the root of creation.
  —*Ernest Dimnet*

There is one thing stronger than all the armies in the world, and that is an idea whose time has come.
  —*Victor Hugo*

PURPOSE

The secret of success is constancy of purpose.
   —*Benjamin Disraeli*

Great minds have purposes, others have wishes.
   —*Washington Irving*

The fruit that can fall without shaking indeed is too mellow for me.
   —*Lady Mary Wortley Montagu*

The man without a purpose is like a ship without a rudder—a waif, a nothing, a no man. Have a purpose in life, and, having it, throw such strength of mind and muscle into your work as God has given you.
   —*Thomas Carlyle*

The only failure a man ought to fear is failure in cleaving to the purpose he sees to be best.
   —*George Eliot*

The aims of life are the best defense against death.
   —*Primo Levi*

A man with a half-volition goes backwards and forwards, and makes no way on the smoothest road; a man with a whole volition advances on the roughest, and will reach his purpose, if there be even a little wisdom in it.
—*Thomas Carlyle*

There is no road to success but through a clear, strong purpose. Nothing can take its place. A purpose underlies character, culture, position, attainment of every sort.
—*T.T. Munger*

It is an old lesson: a worthy purpose, patient energy for its accomplishment, a resoluteness undaunted by difficulties, and then success.
—*W.M. Punshon*

One great aim like a guiding star, above.
—*Robert Browning*

A man without a purpose is soon down at zero. Better to have a bad purpose than no purpose at all.
—*Thomas Carlyle*

What makes life dreary is the want of a motive.
—*George Eliot*

Purpose is what gives life a meaning.
　　—C.H. Parkhurst

We aim above the mark to hit the mark.
　　—Ralph Waldo Emerson

A good archer is not known by his arrows but his aim.
　　—Thomas Fuller

Childhood may do without a grand purpose, but manhood cannot.
　　—J. G. Holland

However brilliant an action may be, it should not be accounted great when it is not the result of a great purpose.
　　—Francois La Rochefoucauld

He who would arrive at the appointed end must follow a single road and not wander through many ways.
　　—Seneca

When a man does not know what harbor he is making for, no wind is the right wind.
　　—Seneca

The good man is the man who, no matter how morally unworthy he has been, is moving to become better.
   —*John Dewey*

The one prudence in life is concentration, the one evil is dissipation, and it makes no difference whether our dissipations are coarse or fine. Everything is good which takes away one plaything and delusion more, and drives us home to add one stroke of faithful work.
   —*Ralph Waldo Emerson*

A good intention clothes itself with sudden power.
   —*Ralph Waldo Emerson*

He who means well is useless unless he does well.
   —*Plautus*

From a tiny spark comes a great conflagration.
   —*Ben Sirach*

They have sown the wind, and they shall reap a whirlwind.
   —*Book of Hosea*

Many persons have a wrong idea of what constitutes true happiness. It is not attained through self-gratification but through fidelity to a worthy purpose.
        —*Helen Keller*

A man should have any number of little aims about which he should be conscious and for which he should have names, but he should have neither name for, nor consciousness concerning, the main aim of his life.
        —*Samuel Butler*

Good purposes should be the directors of good actions, not the apology for bad.
        —*Thomas Fuller*

Men, like nails, lose their usefulness when they lose direction and begin to bend.
        —*Walter Savage Landor*

The great and glorious masterpiece of man is to know how to live to purpose.
        —*Michel Eyquem de Montaigne*

Obstacles cannot crush me / Every obstacle yields to stern resolve / He who is fixed to a star does not change his mind.
        —*Leonardo da Vinci*

There is one quality more important than know-how, and we cannot accuse the United States of any undue amount of it. This is "know-what," by which we determine not only how to accomplish our purposes, but what our purposes are to be.
—*Norbert Wiener*

A windmill is eternally at work to accomplish one end, although it shifts with every variation of the weather-cock, and assumes ten different positions in a day.
—*Charles C. Colton*

The soul that has no established aim loses itself.
—*Michel Eyquem de Montaigne*

Effort

The bitter and the sweet come from the outside, the hard from within, from one's own efforts.
—*Albert Einstein*

Try first thyself, and after call in God; / For to the worker God himself lends aid.
—*Euripides*

He that would have the fruit must climb the tree.
     —*Thomas Fuller*

Few things are impossible to diligence and skill.
     —*Samuel Johnson*

When we do the best that we can, we never know
what miracle is wrought in our life, or in the life of
another.
     —*Helen Keller*

The struggle alone pleases us, not the victory.
     —*Blaise Pascal*

Life has not taught me to expect nothing, but she has
taught me not to expect success to be the inevitable result of my endeavors. She taught me to seek sustenance
from the endeavor itself, but to leave the result to God.
     —*Alan Paton*

No one knows what he can do till he tries.
     —*Publilius*

To travel hopefully is a better thing than to arrive, and
the true success is to labor.
     —*Robert Louis Stevenson*

It is hard to fail, but it is worse never to have tried to succeed. In this life we get nothing save by effort.
—*Theodore Roosevelt*

The law of nature rules that energy cannot be destroyed. You change its form from coal to steam, from steam to power in the turbine, but you do not destroy energy. In the same way, another law governs human activity and rules that honest effort cannot be lost, but that some day the proper benefits will be forthcoming.
—*Paul Speicher*

Freedom from effort in the present merely means that there has been effort stored up in the past.
—*Theodore Roosevelt*

Many a man never fails because he never tries.
—*Norman MacEwan*

God gives every bird his worm, but He does not throw it into the nest.
—*P.D. James*

There's no taking trout with dry breeches.
—*Miguel de Cervantes*

There is no limit to what a man can do so long as he does not care a straw who gets the credit for it.
    —*C.E. Montague*

Effort is only effort when it begins to hurt.
    —*José Ortega y Gasset*

Everyone confesses in the abstract that exertion which brings out all the powers of body and mind is the best thing for us all; but practically most people do all they can to get rid of it, and as a general rule nobody does much more than circumstances drive them to do.
    —*Harriet Beecher Stowe*

There is no trade or employment but the young man following it may become a hero.
    —*Walt Whitman*

By the work one knows the workman.
    —*Jean La Fontaine*

It is work which gives flavor to life.
    —*Henri-Frederic Amiel*

Don't worry and fret, faint-hearted, / The chances have just begun. / For the best jobs haven't been started, / The best work hasn't been done.
—*Berton Braley*

Work is the grand cure for all the maladies and miseries that ever beset mankind—honest work, which you intend getting done.
—*Robert Browning*

Blessed is he who has found his work; let him ask no other blessedness.
—*Thomas Carlyle*

Honor lies in honest toil.
—*Grover Cleveland*

There is no substitute for hard work.
—*Thomas A. Edison*

Hard work is the best investment a man can make.
—*Charles M. Schwab*

The sum of wisdom is that the time is never lost that is devoted to work.
—*Ralph Waldo Emerson*

Any man who has a job has a chance.
  —*Elbert Hubbard*

Work is the sustenance of noble minds.
  —*Seneca*

Thank God every morning when you get up that you have something to do that day which must be done whether you like it or not. Being forced to work, and forced to do your best, will breed in you temperance and self-control, diligence and strength of will, cheerfulness and content, and a hundred virtues which the idle will never know.
  —*Charles Kingsley*

Great is work which lends dignity to man.
  —*Babylonian Talmud*

I'm a great believer in luck, and I find the harder I work the more I have of it.
  —*Thomas Jefferson*

When people are serving, life is no longer meaningless.
  —*John Gardner*

Work is love made visible.
   —*Kahlil Gibran*

Labor disgraces no man, but occasionally men disgrace labor.
   —*Ulysses S. Grant*

It is better to wear out than to rust out.
   —*Richard Cumberland*

RESPONSIBILITY

Responsibility is the thing people dread most of all. Yet it is the one thing in the world that develops us, gives us manhood or womanhood fiber.
   —*Frank Crane*

Responsibility educates.
   —*Wendell Phillips*

Responsibility is the price of greatness.
   —*Winston Churchill*

You will find men who want to be carried on the shoulders of others, who think that the world owes them a living. They don't seem to see that we must all lift together and pull together.
—*Henry Ford II*

Few things help an individual more than to place responsibility upon him, and to let him know that you trust him.
—*Booker T. Washington*

I believe that every right implies a responsibility; every opportunity, an obligation; every possession, a duty.
—*John D. Rockefeller Jr.*

To let oneself be bound by a duty from the moment you see it approaching is part of the integrity that alone justifies responsibility.
—*Dag Hammarskjöld*

The ability to accept responsibility is the measure of the man.
—*Roy L. Smith*

Man must cease attributing his problems to his environment and learn again to exercise his will, his responsibility, in the realm of faith and morals.
—*Albert Schweitzer*

If each one sweeps in front of his own door, the whole street is clean.
 —*Anonymous*

When one link snaps, the whole chain collapses.
 —*Anonymous*

We are responsible for actions performed in response to circumstances for which we are not responsible.
 —*Allan Massie*

Our main business is not to see what lies dimly at a distance, but to do what clearly lies at hand.
 —*Thomas Carlyle*

We are Goddes stewardes all, noughte of our own we bare.
 —*Thomas Chatterton*

There can be no stable and balanced development of the mind apart from the assumption of responsibility.
 —*John Dewey*

The vast majority of persons of our race have a natural tendency to shrink from the responsibility of standing and acting alone.
 —*Francis Galton*

No matter how lofty you are in your department, the responsibility for what your lowliest assistant is doing is yours.
    —*Bessie R. James and Mary Waterstreet*

Unto whom much is given, of him shall be much required.
    —*The Bible, Luke 12:48*

Liberty means responsibility. That is why most men dread it.
    —*George Bernard Shaw*

The most important thought I ever had was that of my individual responsibility to God.
    —*Daniel Webster*

All men, if they work not as in the great taskmaster's eye, will work wrong, and work unhappily for themselves and for you.
    —*Thomas Carlyle*

Nothing keeps alive the sense of the unworthiness of a life going to waste like the thought of God's watchful eye. Nor is there anything to tone up the honesty of men like the remembrance of personal accountability.
    —*Monday Club Sermons*

Responsibility walks hand in hand with capacity and power.
    —J. G. Holland

Responsibility, n. A detachable burden easily shifted to the shoulders of God, Fate, Fortune, Luck, or one's neighbor. In the days of astrology, it was customary to unload it upon a star.
    —Ambrose Bierce

One can pass on responsibility, but not the discretion that goes with it.
    —Benvenuto Cellini

Everybody's business is nobody's business.
    —English Proverb

Our privileges can be no greater than our obligations. The protection of our rights can endure no longer than the performance of our responsibilities.
    —John F. Kennedy

To be a man precisely, be responsible.
    —Antoine de Saint-Exupery

The fault, dear Brutus, is not in our stars, / But in ourselves, that we are underlings.
   —*Shakespeare*

A burden in the bush is worth two on your hands.
   —*James Thurber*

Responsibility's like a string we can only see the middle of. Both ends are out of sight.
   —*William McFee*

Responsibility is to oneself, and the highest form of it is irresponsibility to oneself, which is to say the calm acceptance of whatever responsibility to others and things comes along.
   —*John Cage*

Though the wisdom or virtue of one can very rarely make many happy, the folly or vice of one man often make many miserable.
   —*Samuel Johnson*

CIRCUMSTANCES

Man is not the creature of circumstances. Circumstances are the creatures of men.
   —*Benjamin Disraeli*

Our first mistake is the belief that the circumstance gives the joy which we give to the circumstance.
  —*Ralph Waldo Emerson*

I am myself plus my circumstance, and if I do not save it, I cannot save myself.
  —*José Ortega y Gasset*

If all our happiness is bound up entirely in our personal circumstances, it is difficult not to demand of life more than it has to give.
  —*Bertrand Russell*

The people who get on in this world are the people who get up and look for the circumstances they want and, if they can't find them, make them.
  —*George Bernard Shaw*

I make the most of all that comes, / And the least of all that goes.
  —*Sara Teasdale*

If things go wrong, don't go with them.
  —*Roger W. Babson*

I endeavor to subdue circumstances to myself, and not myself to circumstances.
  —*Horace*

It is not circumstances in which we are placed, but the spirit in which we meet them that constitutes our comfort.
    —*Elizabeth T. King*

I have learned, in whatever state I am, to be content.
    —*The Bible, Philippians 4:11*

Circumstances are beyond the control of man, but his conduct is in his own power.
    —*Benjamin Disraeli*

You think me the child of my circumstances: I make my circumstance.
    —*Ralph Waldo Emerson*

Under all this running sea of circumstance, whose waters ebb and flow with perfect balance, lies the aboriginal abyss of real Being.
    —*Ralph Waldo Emerson*

The necessity of circumstances proves friends and detects enemies.
    —*Epictetus*

Circumstances never made the man do right who
didn't do right in spite of them.
   —*Coulson Kernahan*

Circumstances are things round about; we are in them,
not under them.
   —*W.S. Landor*

The circumstances of others seem good to us, while
ours seem good to others.
   —*Publilius*

Breasts the blows of circumstance.
   —*Alfred Tennyson*

Circumstances are not beyond my individual control.
   —*Charles Dickens*

There are moments when you feel free, moments
when you have energy, moments when you have hope,
but you can't rely on any of these things to see you
through. Circumstances do that.
   —*Anita Brookner*

It always remains true that if we had been greater, circumstance would have been less strong against us.
    —*George Eliot*

Fortuitous circumstances constitute the molds that shape the majority of human lives, and the hasty impress of an accident is too often regarded as the relentless decree of all-ordaining fate.
    —*Augusta Jane Evans*

A merciless fate threw me into this maelstrom. I wanted much, I began much, but the gale of the world carried away me and my work.
    —*Draza Mihajlovic*

Necessity is an evil, but there is no necessity for continuing to live subject to necessity.
    —*Epicurus*

Nothing has more strength than dire necessity.
    —*Euripides*

The true creator is necessity, who is the mother of our invention.
    —*Plato*

Man cannot be free if he does not know that he is subject to necessity, because his freedom is always won in his never wholly successful attempts to liberate himself from necessity.
—*Hannah Arendt*

Necessity hath no law.
—*Oliver Cromwell*

We do what we must, and call it by the best names.
—*Ralph Waldo Emerson*

I do not believe in a fate that falls on men however they act, but I do believe in a fate that falls on them unless they act.
—*G.K. Chesterton*

Fate, then, is a name for facts not yet passed under the fire of thought, for causes which are unpenetrated.
—*Ralph Waldo Emerson*

We are not permitted to choose the frame of our destiny. But what we put into it is ours.
—*Dag Hammarskjöld*

No cause has he to say his doom is harsh, / Who's made the master of his destiny.
   —*Friedrich Von Schiller*

Lots of folks confuse bad management with destiny.
   —*Ken Hubbard*

Destiny is no matter of chance. It is a matter of choice. It is not a thing to be waited for; it is a thing to be achieved.
   —*William Jennings Bryan*

CHARACTER

A character is like an acrostic: read it forward, backward, or across, it still spells the same thing.
   —*Ralph Waldo Emerson*

It is well for the world that in most of us, by the age of thirty, the character has set like plaster and will never soften again.
   —*William James*

It is fortunate to be of high birth, but it is no less so to be of such character that people do not care to know whether you are or are not.
    —*Jean de La Bruyère*

In this world a man must either be anvil or hammer.
    —*Henry Wadsworth Longfellow*

You can tell a lot about a fellow's character by his way of eating jelly beans.
    —*Ronald Reagan*

Character is the basis of happiness, and happiness the sanction of character.
    —*George Santayana*

The best index to a person's character is (a) how he treats people who can't do him any good, and (b) how he treats people who can't fight back.
    —*Abigail Van Buren*

Our characters are the result of our conduct.
    —*Aristotle*

Character: a reserved force which acts directly by presence and without means.
    —*Ralph Waldo Emerson*

Character is higher than intellect. . . . A great soul will be strong to live, as well as to think.
    —*Ralph Waldo Emerson*

Character, that sublime health which values one moment as another, and makes us great in all conditions.
    —*Ralph Waldo Emerson*

A great character . . . is a dispensation of Providence, designed to have not merely an immediate, but a continuous, progressive, and never-ending agency. It survives the man who possessed it; survives his age, perhaps his country, his language.
    —*Edward Everett*

Character is Destiny.
    —*Heraclitus*

Character is simply habit long continued.
    —*Plutarch*

Character is like a tree, and reputation like its shadow. The shadow is what we think of it; the tree is the real thing.
    —*Abraham Lincoln*

Character is what you are in the dark.
—*Dwight L. Moody*

Character is the governing element of life, and is
above genius.
—*Frederick Saunders*

It is energy, the central element of which is will, that
produces the miracles of enthusiasm in all ages.
Everywhere it is the mainspring of what is called force
of character, and the sustaining power of all great
action.
—*Samuel Smiles*

Character is not made in a crisis; it is only exhibited.
—*Robert Freeman*

Instead of saying that a man is the creature of circumstance, it would be nearer the mark to say that man is
the architect of circumstance. It is character which
builds an existence out of circumstance. From the same
materials one man builds palaces, another hovels; one
warehouses, another villas; bricks and mortar are mortar and bricks until the architect can make them something else.
—*Thomas Carlyle*

The four cornerstones of character on which the structure of this nation was built are initiative, imagination, individuality, and independence.
—*Edward Rickenbacker*

Character is not in the mind. It is in the will.
—*Fulton J. Sheen*

The character of Jesus has not only been the highest pattern of virtue, but the strongest incentive to its practice, and has exerted so deep an influence that it may be truly said that the simple record of his three short years of active life has done more to regenerate and soften mankind than all the disquisitions of philosophers and the exhortations of moralists.
—*William Lecky*

What you dislike in another, take care to correct in yourself.
—*Thomas Sprat*

If your absence doesn't make any difference, your presence won't either.
—*Anonymous*

When God measures a man, he puts the tape around the heart, not around the head.
—*Anonymous*

A man is what he thinks about all day long.
—*Ralph Waldo Emerson*

History is the record of an encounter between character and circumstance.
—*Donald Creighton*

Even polished brass will pass upon more people than rough gold.
—*Earl of Chesterfield*

No man knows of what stuff he is made until prosperity and ease try him.
—*A.P. Gouthey*

Integrity has no need of rules.
—*Albert Camus*

During my eighty-seven years, I have witnessed a whole succession of technological revolutions. But none of them has done away with the need for character in the individual or the ability to think.
—*Bernard Baruch*

The measure of a man's real character is what he would do if he knew he never would be found out.
—*Thomas Babington Macaulay*

FAITH

Strike from mankind the principle of faith, and men would have no more history than a flock of sheep.
—*Henry Bulwer*

Faith makes the uplook good, the outlook bright, the inlook favorable, and the future glorious.
—*V. Raymond Edman*

Faith is a living, daring confidence in God's grace. It is so sure and certain that a man could stake his life on it a thousand times.
—*Martin Luther*

Faith makes things possible; it does not make them easy.
—*Anonymous*

Faith is the final triumph over incongruity, the final assertion of the meaningfulness of existence.
—*Reinhold Niebuhr*

Faith is the sight of the inward eye.
—*Alexander Maclaren*

Faith is a resting of the heart in the sufficiency of the evidences.
   —*Clark Pinnock*

The smallest seed of faith is better than the largest fruit of happiness.
   —*Henry David Thoreau*

When faith is lost, when honor dies, the man is dead.
   —*John Greenleaf Whittier*

It's not dying for faith that's so hard; it's living up to it.
   —*William Makepeace Thackeray*

Now faith is being sure of what we hope for and certain of what we do not see.
   —*Apostle Paul*

Faith is love taking the form of aspiration.
   —*William Ellery Channing*

Faith may be defined briefly as an illogical belief in the occurrence of the improbable.
   —*H.L. Mencken*

Everything is possible for him who believes.
    —*Jesus*

Faith is not a thing which one loses; we merely cease
to shape our lives by it.
    —*Georges Bernanos*

For verily I say unto you, that whosoever shall say
unto this mountain, be thou removed, and be thou cast
into the sea; and shall not doubt in his heart, but shall
believe that those things which he saith shall come to
pass; he shall have whatsoever he saith.
    —*Jesus*

What is faith but a kind of betting or speculation after
all? It should be, I bet that my Redeemer liveth.
    —*Samuel Butler*

Faith is the Pierless Bridge / Supporting what We see /
Unto the Scene that We do not.
    —*Emily Dickinson*

Reason is our soul's left hand, / Faith her right, / By
these we reach divinity.
    —*John Donne*

Our faith is faith in someone else's faith, and in the greatest matters this is most the case.
—*William James*

Faith is the highest passion in a human being. Many in every generation may not come that far, but none comes further.
—*Oliver Wendell Holmes*

Back of every creation, supporting it like an arch, is faith. Enthusiasm is nothing: it comes and goes. But if one believes, then miracles occur.
—*Henry Miller*

It is as absurd to argue men as to torture them into believing.
—*Cardinal John Newman*

Faith certainly tells us what the senses do not, but not the contrary of what they see; it is above, not against them.
—*Blaise Pascal*

It is the heart which perceives God and not the reason. That is what faith is: God perceived by the heart, not by the reason.
—*Blaise Pascal*

Faith is an excitement and an enthusiasm: it is a condition of intellectual magnificence to which we must cling as to a treasure, and not squander on our way through life in the small coin of empty words, or in exact and priggish argument.
  —*George Sand*

Despotism may govern without faith, but liberty cannot. . . . How is it possible that society should escape destruction if the moral tie is not strengthened in proportion as the political tie is relaxed? And what can be done with a people who are their own masters if they are not submissive to the Deity?
  —*Alexis de Tocqueville*

Philosophic argument, especially that drawn from the vastness of the universe, in comparison with the apparent insignificance of this globe, has sometimes shaken my reason for the faith that is in me; but my heart has always assured and reassured me that the gospel of Jesus Christ must be Divine Reality. The Sermon on the Mount cannot be a mere human production. This belief enters into the very depth of my conscience. The whole history of man proves it.
  —*Daniel Webster*

The mysteries of faith are degraded if they are made into an object of affirmation and negation, when in reality they should be an object of contemplation.
  —*Simone Weil*

Faith does not become its own object, that produces fanaticism; but it becomes the means whereby God unveils His purposes to us.
    —*Oswald Chambers*

Faith is built on heroism.
    —*Oswald Chambers*

The business of faith is to convert Truth into reality.
    —*Oswald Chambers*

BALANCE

There is a time for everything, and a season for every activity under Heaven: a time to be born and a time to die, a time to plant and a time to uproot, a time to kill and a time to heal, a time to tear down and a time to build, a time to weep and a time to laugh, a time to mourn and a time to dance, a time to scatter stones and a time to gather them, a time to embrace and a time to refrain, a time to search and a time to give up, a time to keep and a time to throw away, a time to tear and a time to mend, a time to be silent and a time to speak, a time to love and a time to hate, a time for war and a time for peace.
    —*The Bible, Ecclesiastes 3:1*

True happiness can only be achieved by living a balanced life.
—*Glenn Bland*

Balance *(noun)*: To bring into or keep in equal or satisfying proportion or harmony.
—*The American Heritage Dictionary*
   of the English Language

Index

A

Aaron as God's spokesperson
  to Pharaoh, 83
Adversity
  belief in purpose for over-
    coming, 28
  luminaries' view of, 25–26
  overcoming, 24–25
Aesop, reward of effort in fable
  of, 31–32
Allen, James, 116
American Heritage Dictionary of
  the English Language, 154
American society, opportunities
  for individuals in, 9–10
Amiel, Henri-Frederic, 128
Amway Corporation, birth of,
  4–5
Applewhite, Scott, drug dealing
  of, 21–23
Arendt, Hannah, 141
Aristotle, 143
Ashley, Timothy, 38–39
Avarice, 49

B

Babson, Roger W., 138
Bachelard, Gaston, 115
Balance, 97–109
  character in, 107
  quotations about, 153–54

Baruch, Bernard, 147
Benham, W. G., 117
Bernanos, Georges, 150
Bible as guideline for effort, 33
Bierce, Ambrose, 135
Bland, Glenn, 154
Bloodworth, Venice, 116
Book of Hosea, 123
Boorstin, Daniel J., 115
Braley, Berton, 117, 129
Brookner, Anita, 140
Browning, Robert, 121, 129
Bryan, William Jennings, 142
Bulwer, Henry, 148
Butler, Samuel, 124, 150

C

Cage, John, 136
Camus, Albert, 147
Careers of successful
  dreamers, 3
Carlyle, Thomas, 120–21, 129,
  133, 134, 145
Carpenter of Nazareth. See Jesus
Cellini, Benvenuto, 135
Cervantes, Miguel de, 127
Chambers, Oswald, 153
Chambliss, Jerry, sales career
  of, 52–54
Change
  agents of, 58
  as necessary for growth, 57
Channing, William Ellery, 149

Character, 67–75
    acquiring great, 72–73
    decrease in citizenry of,
        67–68
    influence on everything
        of, 71
    integration of acts and, 68
    man as architect of his
        own, 73
    need of, 75
    quotations about, 142–47
    time for, 107
Chatterton, Thomas, 133
Chesterton, G. K., 141
Churchill, Winston
    reading quotations advo-
        cated by, 113
    responsibility described by,
        50, 131
Circumstances, 51–65
    attacking cause of bad, 58
    controllable, 51–52
    improving, 58–59
    man as creator of his, 61,
        71–72, 106–7
    obstruction of accomplish-
        ment by, 54
    outward, 61–62
    quotations about, 137–42
    as stepping stones to
        destiny, 65
    thoughts as creating, 55
    time for, 106–7
    uncontrollable, 51, 56
    will as creating, 57
Cleveland, Grover, 129
Clulow, Joseph, 116
Colton, Charles C., 125
Commitment to success, 25, 47
    personal progress as begin-
        ning with, 54
    transforming personal, 59

Constructive thinking as real
    business of life, 32
Crane, Frank, 131
Creighton, Donald, 147
Cromwell, Oliver, 141
Cumberland, Richard, 131

D

David, relationship with God
    of, 79–80
Davies, Robertson, 115
de La Bruyäre, Jean, 143
Desire
    created by dreams, 101
    to succeed, 47
Destiny
    changing your, 64–65
    choosing your own, 58
De Vos, Richard, 4, 14
Dewey, John, 123, 133
Dickens, Charles, 139
Dickinson, Emily, 150
Diligence of, 33–34, 38–39
Dimnet, Ernest, 119
Disraeli, Benjamin, 118, 120,
    137, 138
Donne, John, 150
Doubt as disabling condition,
    27–28
Dreams, 3–17
    achievements as seeds of, 13
    actions spurred on by,
        97–98
    concentrated effort required
        to achieve, 39
    educational dreams, 102
    financial, 100–101
    focus on, 24
    getting and holding, 16
    held dear, 12, 58

pursuit of, examples of,
6–7, 54
quotations about, 114–19
recreational, 102–4
spiritual, 99–100
time for, 98–99
translated into purpose, 4, 19,
23, 104

E

Earl of Chesterfield, 147
Earls, F. Robert, sales career of,
35–36
Ecclesiastes, balance described
in, 97
Edison, Thomas A., 129
Edman, V. Raymond, 148
Educational dreams, 102
Effort, 31–39
essence of, 32
to fulfill dreams, 39
importance of diligent,
33–34, 38–39
material reward as product
of, 31
quotations about, 125–31
success from, 49
time for, 105
Einstein, Albert, 125
Eliot, George, 120, 121, 140
Emerson, Ralph Waldo
character described by,
142–44, 147
circumstances described by,
51, 137, 138–39, 141
dreams described by,
116–18
effort described by, 129
purpose described by,
122, 123

Energy generated by having
purpose, 23–24, 104
Epictetus, 139
Epicurus, 140
Equal opportunity in America,
Martin Luther King, Jr.'s
work toward, 5–7
Euripides, 125, 140
Evans, Augusta Jane, 140
Everett, Edward, 144
Evil rewarded by evil, 64

F

Faith, 77–96
defined by the Apostle
Paul, 77
empowerment phase of,
88–90
focusing of, 92, 95, 108
idea phase of, 85–87
in the infinite versus the
finite, 78–79
of Moses, 89–90
patience phase of, 90–93
quotations about, 148–53
reward phase of, 93
slow growth of, 81
testing phase of, 87–88
time for, 107–9
unconditional, 79
Falkland Islands, Great Britain
and Argentina's war over,
11–12
Fear
as disabling condition, 27–28
falling prey to, 57
Financial dreams, 100–101
Fitzgerald, F. Scott, 115
Ford, Henry, 117
Ford, Henry, II, 132

Foster, Vincent, focus of faith
for, 78
Freeman, Robert, 145
Fuller, Thomas, 122, 124, 126

G

Galton, Francis, 133
Gardner, John, 130
Gentry, Cornelius, unfavorable
circumstances of, 59
Getty, J. Paul
search for oil of, 19–20
as world's first billionaire, 21
Gibran, Kahlil, 131
Goals, turning dreams into,
99–100, 109
God
communication through
prayer with, 80–81
Moses chosen to lead
Israelites from Egypt by,
81–85
oneness with, 99–100
placing faith in, 78, 80
preeminent character of, 79
wisdom of *Homo sapiens*
granted by, 81
Goddard, Robert H., 119
Goethe, Johann Wolfgang von, 98
Good rewarded by good, 64
Gouthy, A. P., 147
Grant, Ulysses S., 131
Growth
cause and effect for
personal, 72
change as necessary for, 57
Moses' change as example
of personal, 84
positive contribution of misfortune to personal, 62

H

Hammarskjold, Dag, 132, 142
Hazlitt, William, 117
Heraclitus, 144
Higher Law
denying existence of, 64
responsible people favored
by, 48–49
rules of, 41
Holland, J. G., 41, 122, 135
Holmes, Oliver Wendall
faith described by, 151
growth of ideas described
by, 85
Honesty, 61–62
Horace, 138
Hubbard, Elbert, 130, 142
Hugo, Victor, 119
Huneker, James, 117

I

Indecisiveness as disabling
condition, 27–28
Irving, Washington, 19, 120
Israelites
escape from Egypt of,
81–85
phases of faith for Moses
and, 85–94

J

James, Bessie R., 134
James, P. D., 127
James, William
character described
by, 142
faith described by, 77, 151

Jefferson, Thomas
   effort described by, 130
   existence of God described
     by, 108–9
Jepson, R. W., 118
Jesus
   cause and effect for, 75
   commitment of, 25
   dreams described by, 118
   great dream of, 23
   mission of, 13–14
   power of belief described
     by, 150
   power of faith illustrated by,
     95–96
   view of good and bad minds
     of, 57
Johnson, Samuel, 126, 136

K

Keller, Helen, 124, 126
Kennedy, John F., 135
Kernahan, Coulson, 139
King, Elizabeth T., 138
King, Martin Luther, Jr.
   uniqueness of people seen
     by, 9
   vision of, 10, 115
   work for equal opportunity
     of, 5–7
Kingsley, Charles, 130
Knowledge, types of, 102

L

La Fontaine, Jean, 128
La Rochefoucauld,
   Francois, 122
Landor, Walter Savage, 124, 139

Law of Cause and Effect, 15, 64
   character and, 68, 71, 73, 75
   example of Israelites for, 92
Lecky, William, 146
Leisure, excessive, 34
Leonardo da Vinci, 124
Levi, David, lifestyle of, 59–60
Levi, Primo, 120
Lincoln, Abraham, 144
Locke, John, character
   described by, 67
Longfellow, Henry Wadsworth
   character described by, 143
   effort described by, 38
Lowell, J. R., 117
Luke, responsibility described
   in, 134
Luminaries of the world, com-
   mon threads among,
   25–26
Luther, Martin, 148
Lyons, Jeremy Q.
   business and personal
     decline of, 43–44
   turn around in computer
     sales of, 44–46

M

Macaulay, Thomas Babington, 147
MacEwan, Norman, 127
McFee, William, 136
Maclaren, Alexander, 148
Massie, Allan, 133
Mencken, H. L., 149
Mihajlovic, Draza, 140
Miller, Arthur, 119
Miller, Henry, 151
Minds
   cultivation of, 8
   illustration of function of, 55

Misfortune, cause of, 62–63
Monday Club Sermons, 134
Montagu, Mary Wortley, 120
Montaigne, Michel Eyquem de,
    124, 125
Montapert, Alfred Armand, 116
Montegue, C. E., 128
Moody, Dwight L., 145
Moses
    empowerment phase of, 88–90
    faith of, 89–90
    God's people led from Egypt
        by, 81–85
    idea phase for, 85–87
    patience phase of, 90–93
    reward phase of, 93–94
    testing phase of, 87–88
Munger, T. T., 121

N

Namath, (Broadway) Joe, 32–33
Newman, John, 151
Niebuhr, Reinhold, 148

O

Obstacles. *See* Adversity
Ortega y Gasset, José, 128, 137
O'Sheel, Sharmas, 3

P

Pain barrier, breaking, 26–27
Parkhurst, C. H., 122
Pascal, Blaise, 126, 151
Paton, Alan, 126
Paul (Saul), faith defined by,
    77, 149

Peter, Jesus' test of faith of, 95–96
Philippians, circumstances
    described in, 138
Phillips, Wendell, 131
Pinnock, Clark, 149
Plato, 118, 141
Plautus, 123
Plutarch, 144
Practice, greatness as recom-
    pense for, 29
Pritchard, Keith W., sales career
    of, 35–36
Procter, Adalaide Ann, 117
Prosperity, preparing for, 9
Proverbs, dreams described in, 114
Publilius, 126, 139
Punshon, W. M., 121
Purpose, 19–29
    challenges of definitive, 28
    as compass for journey of
        life, 29
    dreams translated into, 4, 19,
        23, 104
    energy from having sense
        of, 23–24, 104
    example of lack of, 21–23
    of luminaries of the world,
        25–26
    made a priority, 24–25
    quotations about, 120–25
    satisfaction of accomplish-
        ing, 32–33
    time for, 104

Q

Quotations, classic, 111–54
    about balance, 153–54
    about character, 142–47
    about circumstances, 137–42
    about dreams, 114–19
    about effort, 125–31

about faith, 148–53
about purpose, 120–25
about responsibility, 131–36

R

Reagan, Ronald, 143
Recreational dreams, 102–4
Relativism as guide for
    behavior, 67
Responsibility, 41–50
    accepting, 41–42, 46–47, 63
    outcomes of, 50
    quotations about, 131–36
    time for, 105–6
    usurped by rulers and
        governments, 47
Responsible living, rules for, 42
Rickenbacker, Edward, 146
Rockefeller, John D., Jr., 132
Roosevelt, Theodore
    effort described by, 127, 128
    vision of, 15
Russell, Bertrand, 137

S

Sabbath, rest and renewal on,
    33–34, 36–37, 54
Sacrifice, personal, 59
Saint-Exupery, Antoine de, 135
Sand, George, 152
Santayana, George, 143
Saunders, Frederick, 145
Schwab, Charles M., 129
Schweitzer, Albert, 19, 132
Self-esteem, healthy, 50
Self-renewal, necessity of, 37
Seneca, 122, 130
Shakespeare, William, 136

Shaw, George Bernard, 115,
    134, 137
Sheen, Fulton J., 146
Sirach, Ben, 123
Smiles, Samuel, 145
Smith, Roy L., 132
Smith, Theodore Chadick,
    Law of Cause and Effect
    for, 68–71
Socialism, 11
Solomon
    balance described by, 153
    circumstances and thoughts
        described by, 72
    diligence described by, 38
    prosperity described by, 31
Speicher, Paul, 127
Spiritual dreams, 99–100
Spiritual Law, 100
Sprat, Thomas, 146
Stevens, Will, discovery of
    silver by, 73–74
Stevenson, Robert Louis, 126
Stowe, Harriet Beecher, 128
Success
    career, 3
    material, outcomes of, 48–49
    purpose as leading to, 25–26
    true, 8, 47, 49–50, 63, 108, 109
Swift, Jonathan, 116

T

Talmud (Babylonia), 130
Teasdale, Sara, 138
Ten Commandments
    revelation to Moses of,
        84–85, 91
    as rules for responsible
        living, 42
Tennyson, Alfred, 139

Testing, withstanding, 88
Thackeray, William
        Makepeace, 149
Thatcher, Margaret
    dream of, 12
    monetary policy of, 11–12
    rise of, 10–11
Thoreau, Henry David, 119, 149
Thought
    as agent of change, 58
    circumstances created by, 55
    imaginative, laboriousness
        of, 32
    power of, 1–109
    true success as handiwork of
        principled, 8, 49–50
Thurber, James, 136
Time
    for character, 107
    for circumstances, 106–7
    for effort, 105
    for faith, 107–9
    for purpose, 104
    for responsibility, 105–6
Tocqueville, Alexis de, 152

U

Updike, John, 116

V

Van Andel, Jay, 4
Van Buren, Abigail, 143
Vision
    in dreams, 3–17
    as signet of destiny, 17
Von Schiller, Johann Friedrich,
        118, 142

W

Washington, Booker T., 132
Waterstreet, Mary, 134
Webster, Daniel, 134, 152
Weil, Simone, 152
Whitman, Walt, 128
Whittier, John Greenleaf, 149
Wiener, Norbert, 125
Williams, Benjamin, sales career
        of, 60–61
Wisdom, learning, 67
Working, God's principle of
        human, 33–34

Y

Yager, Dexter, 114